THE
SANTA FE
TRAIL
BY BICYCLE

A TRAVEL GUIDE

He war comin' down the Santa Fe trail
Astride of a wheel with a crooked tail,
A skinnin' along, with a merry song,
An' ringin' a little warnin' gong.

From Broncho vs. Bicycle
(A Nineteenth Century epic poem)
*by Capt. Jack Crawford, the Poet Scout.
Courtesy Museum of New Mexico.*

THE
SANTA FE
TRAIL
BY BICYCLE

A Historic Adventure

A TRAVEL GUIDE by Elaine Pinkerton

R · E · D
CRANE
BOOKS

1993
SANTA FE

To my husband, Robert Hudson Dinegar

First Edition

Manufactured in the United States of America

Contemporary photos by Murrae Haynes

Historic photos courtesy Museum of New Mexico

Maps created by Deborah Reade

Weather charts were made from a publication of the National Oceanic and Atmospheric Administration, compiled from records on file at the National Climatic Data Center, Asheville, North Carolina 28801.

Book design and typography by John Cole

Front cover: Arrival of the caravan at Santa Fe, New Mexico, ca. 1844. Lithograph by E. Didier. Courtesy Museum of New Mexico, Neg. No. 45011. Photo of the author by Murrae Haynes.

Back cover: Detail of bicyclist and his dog in Las Vegas, New Mexico, ca. 1898. Courtesy Museum of New Mexico, Neg. No. 76990.

Pinkerton, Elaine.
    The Santa Fe trail by bicycle : a historic
  adventure / Elaine Pinkerton. — 1st ed.
      p.   cm.
   ISBN 1–878610–24–4
   1. Bicycle touring—Santa Fe Trail—Guidebooks.
  2. Santa Fe Trail—Guidebooks. I. Title.
  GV1045.5.S26P56   1993
  796.6'4'0979—dc20

Red Crane Books
826 Camino de Monte Rey
Santa Fe, New Mexico 87501

CONTENTS

DAILY RIDE SCHEDULE

Day	Town	Miles	km
1	Santa Fe to Las Vegas, N. Mex. 72		115
2	Las Vegas to Wagon Mound, N. Mex. 60		96
3	Wagon Mound to Cimarron, N. Mex. 57		91
4	Cimarron, N. Mex. to Trinidad, Colo. 69		110
5	*Layover Day*		
6	Trinidad to La Junta, Colo. 87		139
7	La Junta to Lamar, Colo. 69		110
8	Lamar, Colo. to Lakin, Kans. 79		126
9	Lakin to Dodge City, Kans. 84		134
10	*Layover Day*		
11	Dodge City to Larned, Kans. 69		110
12	Larned to Sterling, Kans. 56		90
13	Sterling to Hillsboro, Kans. 67		107
14	Hillsboro to Council Grove, Kans. 63		101
15	*Layover Day*		
16	Council Grove to Baldwin City, Kans. 80		128
17	Baldwin City, Kans. to Independence, Mo. .70		112
18	Independence to Lexington, Mo. 45		72
19	Lexington to Arrow Rock, Mo. 57		91
20	Arrow Rock to New Franklin, Mo. 45		72
21	*Recovery Day*		
	TOTAL 1,129		1,804

THE ONE-WEEK PLAN

Taken separately, any one of the above "blocks" will make an enjoyable mini-trek. Willard Chilcott's Santa Fe Trail Bicycle Trek, which leaves every September from Santa Fe, accommodates riders who will be traveling for only a week or two as well as those planning to go the entire distance.

A detail of "goods for export" in Dodge City, Kansas. Photo by J. Lee-knight. Courtesy Museum of New Mexico, Neg. No. 130899.

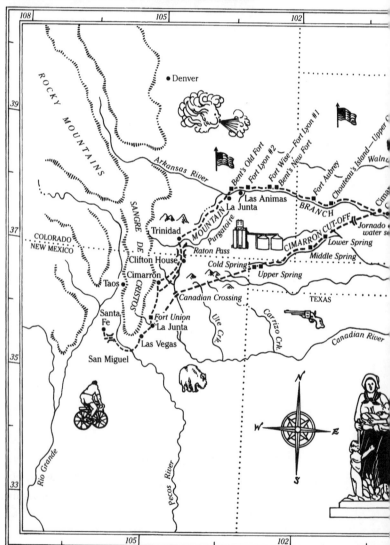

A detail of prairie schooners under convoy, 1830s. Courtesy Museum of New Mexico, Neg. No. 87450.

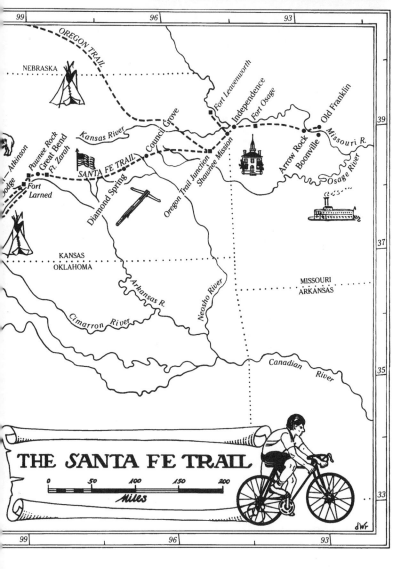

THE SANTA FE TRAIL

0   50   100   150   200
Miles

TEMPERATURE & PRECIPITATION CHARTS

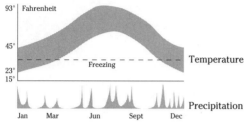

Albuquerque, N.Mex.—For Santa Fe, subtract 5–8 degrees from average temperature.

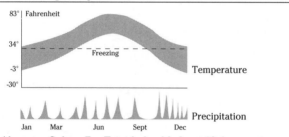

Alamosa, Colo.—For Trinidad, add about 10 degrees to average temperature.

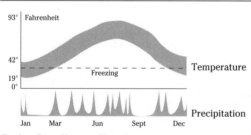

Dodge City, Kans.—Use chart as is.

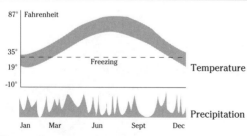

Kansas City, Mo.—Use chart as is.

FOREWORD

Marc Simmons

One of the most dramatic, even romantic, episodes in the history of America's westward movement is the story of old pioneer trails that threaded their way across the heart of the continent, serving as arteries for the circulation of people, animals, and goods. Understandably, in time there accumulated around each trail a trove of tales weighted with excitement, adventure, tragedy, and always some humor. Such are the elements which today account for our lingering fascination with trail history.

Within that field, the Santa Fe Trail occupies a prominent place. It was the first of the great overland paths established west of the Mississippi, running from the then frontier state of Missouri to the distant province of New Mexico on the northern fringe of the Republic of Mexico. And it was the western trail destined to survive the longest period of time, from its opening in 1821 down to the closing in 1880, a span of almost sixty years.

The last quarter of the twentieth century has witnessed a revival of interest in the old trail to Santa Fe. In 1987 Congress elevated it to the status of a National Historic Trail, bringing it under the jurisdiction of the National Park Service for interpretive purposes. That development has led the media to focus its spotlight on the trail, giving it a new place in the public consciousness. Thus more and more people are traveling the Santa Fe Trail these days, seeking out its scenic and historical riches. Most go in comfort by automobile, of course. But some, in search of a more authentic experience, elect to travel by foot, horseback, or wagon.

And then we have those adventurers, strong of limb and lung, who set out to cover the long, long miles of this marvelous trail by bicycle. The rate of locomotion on a two-wheeler is much greater than that of a nineteenth-century ox wagon or stagecoach. But something of the original experience is retained by the bicycle rider who must face sun and weather on the open road and who can only reach trail's end by the exercise of muscle and the summoning of endurance.

Elaine Pinkerton, having done it this way herself, has written a useful guide for bicyclists wishing to accept the challenge of retracing the historic Santa Fe Trail. In these pages will be found both practical information and nuggets of history. So, assemble your gear, give that bike a final check, and let's go exploring on one of America's great trails. ✻

Bicyclist and his dog in Las Vegas, New Mexico, ca. 1898. Courtesy Museum of New Mexico, Neg. No. 76990.

ACKNOWLEDGMENTS

I would like to thank Willard Chilcott, originator of the Santa Fe Trail Bicycle Trek, without whose invitation, encouragement, and practical assistance my discovery of the Santa Fe Trail by bicycle would never have happened. Thanks also to the many kind people who fed and nurtured our cycling group along the trail—the teachers and students of Wagon Mound School, who prepared a splendid enchilada dinner; the senior citizens; Lions Clubs; bicycling clubs; colleges and chambers of commerce; and the hospitable folk of New Franklin, Missouri, who celebrated the successful completion of our trek with a community hog roast.

I'm grateful to my editors, Robert LeCompte and Dennis H. Dutton, for their patience, diligence, and understanding; to the creative efforts of Deborah Reade, the mapmaker for *The Santa Fe Trail by Bicycle;* to Marc Simmons for lending his historical expertise; to Charles Spain Verral, Jr., for reviewing my bicycling tips; and especially to Carol Caruthers of Red Crane Books, whose patience and encouragement were unfailing. ❀

Santa Fe Trail ruts near Fort Union, New Mexico, ca. 1945.
Photo by Harold D. Walter. Courtesy Museum of New Mexico,
Neg. No. 128726.

INTRODUCTION

A bicycle trek on the Santa Fe Trail is a trip through history over a byway so ancient that it may have originated as a game trail. Some trail authorities speculate that buffalo, antelope, deer, and other animals indigenous to the area used parts of the route in seasonal migrations. Indians traveled the trail, and Coronado followed it as early as 1541. The trail's real heyday was roughly from the 1820s through 1880 and the advent of the railroad. In those six decades, the Santa Fe Trail was a highway for traders, pioneers, adventurers, and westward-bound emigrants.

Lieutenant Zebulon M. Pike, in his *Journal of the Western Expedition* (1810), commented that Americans speculated that trade with the Spanish Southwest might be very profitable indeed. Their intuition was correct, and for over half a century the Santa Fe Trail was the path of countless men and women, wagon wheels, and hundreds of thousands of hooves, cloven and uncloven. It became the line of march for an army of aggression. It was a route marked for those who sought a new life, a new fate, a new fortune, the way of adventure, great wealth, life, and romance. The trail's greatest commercial traffic occured in 1855, with some $5 million in profits. By the turn of the century, however, this commercial traffic had been almost totally replaced by the railroad.

The history of the trail is, in large part, the history of the American West. When you embark on this trip—on two wheels rather than in a Conestoga wagon—you will travel this part of our heritage for well over 1,000 miles. You will walk in wagon ruts, view markers, browse in trail museums and historical centers, and talk with today's trail dwellers. As you do, you will gain a new appreciation for the Santa Fe Trail and its place in history.

Hard as it may be to believe, ruts left by the heavy wheels of Santa Fe Trail wagons remain to this day, well over one hundred years later. Some are on private land, and many have been covered by agriculture or urban buildings, but between Santa Fe, New Mexico, and New Franklin, Missouri, many trail ruts—or "swales" as they are also called—have been preserved. Some ruts, particularly in the west, are miles long. Others are short, often protected in lots or parks.

Look for wide depressions, heavily grassed over, in the ground. It was not unusual for wagons to travel four abreast, especially west of Fort Larned. Deeper, narrower ruts will be found where the wagons ascended a ridge or came out of a stream or river. Tracks can vary widely, and most people will tell you that it requires considerable practice to really see them. Be alert for signs by the road announcing ruts, and also ask folks that you might meet in truck stops or village cafes. Seeing these ruts, standing in them, letting the imagination flow as you contemplate their significance, can provide you with some of your trip's best memories.

Even if you are not a history buff, you will see the heartland of America in a way that cannot be provided by car—feeling its weather, viewing close up its fields and trees, lakes, rivers and streams, braving its wind and rain, basking in its sunshine, surviving its interminable prairies, challenging its rolling hills. In your closeness to nature and the elements, you will get to know the trail country—northern New Mexico, Colorado, Kansas, Missouri—intimately. As you travel through the small, friendly towns of these states, you will get to meet the modern-day trail people, those who live in the shadow of history, and to enjoy their hospitality and willingness to share trail lore.

When I told a cyclist friend of my plans to travel through northern New Mexico, Colorado, Kansas and Missouri by bike, she responded, "Why *there*?" Why waste the miles, she asked, in such bleak, dull country? Why not bicycle in the south of France, something exotic, kind, and gentle?

It was not until after I took three weeks of my life to travel by bike through those "wasted miles" that I could really tell her why. The miles were the ones traveled by the early people who first made the western part of our country. The bleakness and difficulty of some of the stretches told the story of the people themselves.

Though often beautiful, the trail was not an easy undertaking. Even in late summer, a relatively benign time of year, our weather was often harsh. Strong headwinds beat us down on many days. The winds, when combined with heat, parched us; the prairies eroded us. The Raton Pass taxed even the strongest of us. Occasional rain, often turning into sleet, the shoulderless roads of Kansas, the obnoxious truck traffic, made the trek seem at times like an Outward Bound mission.

Keep this in mind. I made the entire trip by bike, but nearly half of my group joined our caravan for just a week or two. There is much to be said for doing only one segment a season and possibly spending longer time sightseeing at the forts or other historic sites along the way.

Biking the Santa Fe Trail was biking through history. As my journey progressed, I had a sense of retracing the path of our country's pioneer forebears. I was seeing the same land of those early adventurers in a way that car travelers never could. Like the pioneers, our cycling group was out in the elements around the clock.

The original starting point of the Santa Fe Trail was the little river town of Franklin, Missouri, which is at the end of this guide. Because prevailing winds are eastward and because I live in the west, I chose to begin at the western end of the trail, in Santa Fe, New Mexico. Cyclists beginning from the east will have to follow the guide in reverse. For those unable to take several weeks to cover the trail all at once, the cycling is divided into four sections, corresponding to weeks that can be taken as separate excursions.

We averaged 60 miles a day, and we never knew what weather and terrain awaited us. Certain areas, such as the Raton Pass and the Flint Hills in eastern Kansas, were predictable challenges, but otherwise, we never knew what the terrain would be. Some days we made as many as 80 miles—many times more than the Santa Fe Trail pioneers were able to advance. But like them, we came to regard each day as an adventure.

The main mission of our Santa Fe Trail forerunners was to carry merchandise from one part of the country to another. Our mission was to retrace, as much as possible, their path, to learn about their lives, to relive some of what they might have experienced. As we got deeper into trail country, our appreciation of them grew, as did our ability to see the sometimes elusive trail ruts they left behind.

This book will tell you how to bike safely from Point "A," the Santa Fe Plaza, to Point "B," New Franklin, Missouri. It will provide a blueprint for covering the thousand miles from the end to the origin of the Santa Fe Trail. But even as the maps and suggestions describe the road to follow, they will be merely tried and tested suggestions.

My guide cannot be complete, as by the time it leaves the printer, it will probably already be slightly out of date. What had been a gravel road will have become paved, markers will have been changed, historical sites altered or vandalized. That is why it is important for you to take maps of your own as well as the ones included. It also helps to talk with folks along your way. You will find your own rhythm. Sometimes after an hour or so of cycling, you will want to stop at a roadside truck stand or a fruit stand to take some refreshment and talk with the locals. They will tell you things that no road map can, and they will probably have useful tips on weather and terrain.

A word about the weather. The Santa Fe Trail should be avoided as a cycling route in the winter. The best times of year are late spring, early summer, or early fall. Rainy spells can occur anytime, and when they do, cycling can become not only unpleasant but dangerous. Allow for bad weather by trying to keep a flexible schedule. If you are bicycling with sheets of rain spraying up from every passing car and truck, you cannot be seen by motorists. Use common sense, and stay in truck stops until the weather changes. If it becomes obvious that the entire day will be stormy, your best choice may be to stay over in a motel, bed and breakfast, or protected campsite. The beauty of being marooned anywhere on the Santa Fe Trail is that you can usually find historic sites to visit. After all, the point of your journey is not just getting in the miles by bike but exploring the trail and learning about trail terrain and history.

After bicycling the Santa Fe Trail the first time, you will want to return. And you will, by then, have your own wealth of trail lore. ✳

Wagon train on plaza, Santa Fe, New Mexico, ca. 1873.
Courtesy Museum of New Mexico, Neg. No. 144637.

Before You Go

They're off!

Chapter One

A Guide to Equipment

Entire books could be written about each of the topics I will be discussing in this chapter, but chances are you would rather spend your time bicycling than reading. So this part of *The Santa Fe Trail by Bicycle* will give you enough basic information to

☞ select the right bike and biking accessories,
☞ pack the essential camping equipment, and
☞ bring clothes that are good for both biking and camping.

If you feel like reading more, consult the bibliography at the end of this book or your local library.

HOW TO SELECT A ROAD BIKE

In the weeks ahead, your bike will become more than just a piece of equipment; it can be either your best friend or a painful necessity. That is why your choice of a bicycle is important. It should be of appropriate size, and it should have exactly the components, gearing, wheels, and looks that you desire. Even if you do not care to get involved with all the technical aspects of bicycling, you must do the homework necessary to choose a bike that is right for *you*.

Before starting your search, seek the advice of friends who are experienced cyclists. Join your local bike club and attend meetings. Not only will you be able to gain knowledge from the voices of experience, but you will also no doubt find companions for weekend training jaunts. Seek out those who have gone "road touring" and learn what works for them.

"Why insist on a *road* bike?" you ask. Mountain bikes, though the most popular machines for many first-time buyers, are not what I would recommend for a road trip of 1,000-plus miles. Designed to cope with off-road difficulties, those rugged bikes are getting lighter and more nimble, but they cannot match the bikes designed for long hours on hard-surfaced routes.

A new species of bicycle has recently emerged, called "hybrid" or "all-terrain," among other names. Usually these are like mountain bikes in that they have upright handlebars and three ranges of gearing. However, they have road-bike wheels, with tires varying from as narrow as those on a typical touring bike to as wide as those on a light mountain bike.

You might want to be wary of hybrids, however. Road-bike handlebars, those curious, uncomfortable-looking, dropped-down things, really help in negotiating rolling hills. They let you bend far over on the downward sections of road and sit upright on the rises, thus helping defeat the wind. "Drop" handlebars, as these are called, offer several hand positions for increased comfort and efficiency. If you bend down, even coasting, as you enter a small valley, you can save a lot of the work pedaling up the other side. The upright handlebars of the hybrid bikes do not offer this amenity.

The wind, by the way, whether blowing on you or created by your movement, will be a constant companion. When you are going less than ten miles an hour (twelve is the average speed), the resistance it gives is insignificant. But suddenly at ten miles an hour it accounts for 50 percent of the work. At thirty, it is 90 percent.

Go through the following checklist before you buy, and you won't go wrong.

FIVE-POINT CHECKLIST FOR BUYING THE RIGHT BIKE

1. Consider your cycling goals. Think beyond the Santa Fe Trail trek, and ask yourself if you might want to win a road race or scale precipitous mountain trails. If you long to do both, you may find yourself a two-bike owner.

2. If you are a person who likes to be at the leading edge of technology, you will not be satisfied with anything but a top-of-the-line bike. But if you are the kind of rider who does not worry about maintenance until something breaks down, then you will want good equipment that is basically maintenance-free. It is important to match mind-set with budget; do not compromise too much. You want a bike that you feel confident is right for *you*.

3. Gearing is a very important factor to consider. While "neighborhood" bikes may need only one to three speeds to make getting around easy, you will need more for serious touring, with its uphills, downhills, level stretches, and transitional zones. The more gears—high to low—the more choices and the easier the pedaling.

Some touring bikes have as few as five, six, or seven speeds, but I strongly recommend choosing one with no fewer than ten or twelve. In fact, it is not at all far-fetched to consider a 21- or 24-speed bicycle; some experts contend that only in these will you find the three to five speeds you will come to rely on most comfortably. The gearing, by the way, is a feature that a dealer can modify fairly inexpensively. If you feel out of shape, or the terrain in your future will be challenging, maybe you will want easier gearing. A good bicycle store can guide you through the technicalities and modify most bikes to have a lower low gear. Very often, the change will be rather inexpensive.

4.   Other changeable features include the seat and toe-clips. If the saddle is too uncomfortable, you can request that it be replaced with a gel-filled model. If you have never used toe-clips, buy them anyway, as they will be essential later. Toe-clips can be removed and—after you are more accustomed to your bike—replaced. The sooner you learn to use them the better. Before my first road bike with toe-clips, I had ridden only a toe-clipless mountain bike. After just a couple falls using the clips, I learned more quickly than I had imagined possible how to use them safely. The clips maximize your pedal power and give you more control.
So-called "clipless" pedals have recently become available which fit into receptacles in special shoes. They are not my choice, but some cyclists prefer them.

5.   Do not buy on your first visit to the bike shop. Review your needs, go to several different shops, and—if the shop allows it—take a test spin on the models you are considering. Talk with the shop owners. Are special orders possible? Make sure that they will they give you the service you desire. Only then will you be assured of ending up with the frame, components, wheels, gearing, and looks best suited to your needs and tastes.
This is also a good time to look over whatever *reasonably new*/used bikes the dealers may have for sale. But do not buy a bargain bike on impulse,

and look with caution on any bike which does not carry a reasonable warranty from the dealer.

INCLUDING THE RIGHT ACCESSORIES

HELMET

The number of riders who are wearing bike helmets seems to be increasing, and for good reason. The saying, "There are only two kinds of riders: those who have had an accident and those who are going to," bears directly on the helmet issue. Good helmets are somewhat expensive, ranging from $40 to $100, but brain cells are irreplaceable.

A well-fitted helmet, some feel, is your number one accessory. When shopping for one, get a sympathetic salesman to check the fit. Test for roll-off by pulling downward on the straps that link under your chin while someone pushes upward on the front edge of the helmet. It should not creep backward, exposing your forehead. Helmets are worn level to the ground, protecting the front as well as the back of the head.

There are two safety-rating systems for protective bicycle headgear: Snell (the Snell Memorial Foundation) and ANSI (the American National Standards Institute). Snell is the more rigorous. A helmet with a sticker stating that it complies with the standards of one of these two organizations is required by most clubs and racing organizations because of insurance requirements. The *Reader's Digest* recently cited that the risk of all head injuries resulting from bicycle accidents could have been reduced by 85% had the riders been wearing helmets.

Current wisdom has it that helmets made of Styrofoam with a thin, slippery cover of plastic offer the most protection. They allow impact-absorption from both inside and out. They tend neither to bounce nor to stick on pavement.

Check with friends who are experienced cyclists to see what brands they consider most protective and comfortable.

QUICK ROAD REPAIR KIT

Flat tires are just part of the road trip, so you need to have a few basics to repair them. Do not wait until you have embarked on the Santa Fe Trail to test your expertise in using them. Practice at home in the garage, or ask your bike dealer to give you some pointers. Nothing replaces hands-on experience. Here is the minimum you will need:

1. *Spare tube(s)*. I prefer having a new, good-quality tube as well as a spare or two that may already have patches. Do not be afraid to ask for advice: your bike dealer can ensure that you have the right valve type and size.

2. *Tire levers*. At least two should be kept in your seat bag. Tough plastic levers work fine, weigh less, and will not jingle as you ride.

3. *Wrenches*. These are needed if your bike has nuts rather than quick-release mechanisms on the wheels. You also need small wrenches for tasks such as adjusting your seat.

4. *Patch kit*. Even if you do have two spare tubes, it is best to have a "better" one that you try to keep intact. The kit should also contain at least ten patches, fine sandpaper or an abrasive instrument, and glue (make sure your glue has not dried up!).

5. *Frame-mount pump*. Make sure that your pump fits your bike and valve stem. The same dealer you buy the bike from will carry this indispensable item.

6. *Seat bag*. These handy items are made to fit semi-permanently under the saddle, usually with hook-and-loop straps. Always keep your repair kit in the bag, and when you venture out, use it for identification, money, keys, and any other small things that you want within easy reach. Seat bags pick up all the dust and grime of the road, so a dark color is best.

Remember that these accessories do you no good unless you are adept at using them. On the road is *not* the ideal place to learn. Practice when you are not being passed by zooming traffic or trying to reach camp by nightfall.

OTHER BIKING ACCESSORIES AND EQUIPMENT

Five Basic Items

You will need to replenish body fluids as you cover the miles, so be sure to equip your bike with a *water bottle* or two and cage(s) to hold them securely onto the frame. Many new bikes come equipped with bottle-cage mounting boots. Be sure that the plastic bottle is held securely.

On long or short trips, a *rearview mirror* is a vital necessity. Some of them fasten on the helmet, and others can be affixed to the handlebars. I feel more comfortable with the helmet style. It will take some adjustment and positioning before you can get the mirror (the helmet style is about the size of a quarter) to actually "pick up" cars behind you. It is an adjustment well worth the time.

Biking shoes, while not absolutely necessary, will go a long way toward increasing your efficiency. Regular shoes will not fit easily in your toe-clips, and the stiff soles of biking shoes will ease your pedaling.

Next to your helmet, *cycling shorts* may well be your most important clothing item. Their long legs protect your inner thighs from chafing, and their chamois or synthetic padded crotch will prove to be a blessing. Basic black is good in that it will go with everything else, but you can also buy bright colors or even loose khaki garments that look more like regular shorts. They are not cheap ($25 to $75), but well worth the expense.

Finally, *padded gloves* will save your hands from numbness, blisters, and rawness. They will also serve as a safeguard against palm lacerations in case of a fall. Starting at about $15, they usually come in a combination of Lycra and leather, often with mesh or terry backs.

Carriers

You will need panniers or carriers to transport your gear. Unless you go with a sag-wagon system (see below), you will want both a front carrier and a pack that fits onto a back bicycle rack or pannier bags that hang over each side of the back tire.

Plan your carriers according to your anticipated travel method. If you do not have a sag wagon and plan to camp out, you will need more carrying space; staying at motels or bed and breakfast inns will allow you to travel lightly.

Easiest is the sag-wagon approach, with a driver to transport your extra clothes, personal items, and camping gear: all you will need during the day is an under-the-seat bag with quick-repair stuff and a front pack for rain gear, windbreaker, snacks, and so forth. However, the sag system does limit your flexibility and freedom. You must accommodate your wishes to those of the group. The choice should be based on the kind of experience you want as well as your level of road-trip expertise. The sag system can give great moral support to the novice road cyclist, and riding in company allows some conversation to brighten the journey.

Whichever method you choose, when you go to the bike shop or peruse catalogues, you will find a vast array of styles and designs in carrying equipment. Shop around for the best equipment.

Once you have purchased your bags, practice riding with them fully packed, remembering that the heaviest items should be placed low and over the hub of the wheel. As mentioned earlier, it is advisable to keep on-the-road, quick-repair equipment in a small bag that fits under the bicycle seat. Contents should include a spare tube, a patch kit, and tire irons. Your bike pump should be attached to the bicycle frame itself. (Recommended is a spare tire, folded neatly and tucked away in one of your larger carriers.) Someone in the group should have repair skills, or at least a well-read manual.

A good rule to remember is *counterbalance*. The double panniers should have balanced loads placed low over both sides of the rear-wheel hub. One bag could contain your tent, if it is small enough, and the other your stove or cook set. The higher you go in the pannier, the lighter the items should be.

Because your sleeping bag and pad will probably not fit into a pannier, they should be strapped *lengthwise* on top of the rear rack. Streamline whenever possible: you will lower wind resistance by not loading crossways.

Try your best to carry no more equipment than you need for sleeping, eating, and biking well on the open road. You can always buy equipment along on the road if you really need it.

Tools

For the long haul, you really should bring the following. If you are traveling with one or more companions, divide up everything except your under-the-seat kit.

- 6-inch adjustable wrench
- brake cable (rear)
- small screwdrivers (Phillips and regular)
- derailleur cable (rear)
- spoke wrench
- chain links
- six spokes with nipples
- brake shoes
- ⁹⁄₁₀- and ⁹⁄₁₀- mm wrenches
- cleaning rag
- tire gauge
- talc for flats (store in labeled film canister)
- appropriate Allen wrenches
- rim strip
- cone wrenches
- crank extractor
- bottom bracket tools
- tube and bicycle grease
- small cable cutters

CAMPING GEAR

With the items discussed above, you will be pretty well set for bicycling itself. But unless you are staying in a hotel or bed-and-breakfast inn every night (some nights there will be very few available), you must also be prepared for camping out. Even if you stay in college dorms or community centers—which can often be arranged by writing ahead, you will still need some camping gear. It is best to try to maintain that carefree "bare biking" feeling as much as possible, so try not to carry more than 35 pounds of equipment. If you are using a sag wagon, it is an entirely different matter; you can keep all but your daytime gear in the truck by day, getting it out only at night.

Your *camping gear* should consist of basically the following:

- water containers
- tent
- tarps and/or ground cloths
- sleeping bag
- foam pad
- knife
- cookstove
- sponge (for tent cleaning and drying)
- matches
- flashlight

A lightweight tent designed especially for carrying on bike trips is highly desirable. Be sure to air and dry it thoroughly before packing it up each morning.

Many of the new "bike light" style tents, which have retractable poles, make up into 12" by 3" packs weighing only a pound or two. The only problem you might have with the retractable poles is that they can get off track and not stretch out properly. In a pinch, I have used a spare spoke as part of a retractable pole system. It is not ideal, but a quick fix that has saved me more than once. Amazing how a few days on the road can bring out your native resourcefulness!

CLOTHING

Clothing is an aspect of your planning and packing that requires close attention, as you will have to live in the same few garments for many days. It is not necessary to spend a fortune, but it is important to choose clothes that you like. Look for fabrics such as polypropylene and Gortex that will "breathe" and protect you from the weather, and plan to pack enough to give you a little variety, be it ever so slight. It is best to "shop" at home first, as you may well be able to adapt what you already have on hand.

A good basic list might include the following:
- cycling shorts
- running shoes, sandals, or moccasins
- cycling shoes
- underwear
- cycling gloves
- long pants
- 2–3 pairs socks
- 2–3 tops
- rain suit (jacket, pants)
- sweatpants
- windbreaker
- hat with brim that protects ears
- lightweight wool sweater

While not absolutely necessary, I recommend choosing for at least one of your shirts the type designed especially for cycling. They have pockets in the back that are handy for snacks, sunglasses, chapstick and other small items, and they can save you having to zip and upzip your front pack too frequently.

MISCELLANEOUS

These items will vary according to your own particular needs and interests, but here are listed the items I have found most useful on road trips.

- vitamins and medication (if needed)
- small first aid kit
- plastic mug or folding cup
- sweatbands (for head, wrists)
- traveler's checks and cash
- glasses retainers (croakies)
- insect repellent
- ziplock plastic bags
- large plastic bag
- towels and washcloths
- bike shorts
- Wash 'n Drys
- extra socks
- sunscreen/lip protection
- dog repellent
- swiss army knife
- sleepwear (long johns work well)
- soap and plastic container
- diary
- shampoo
- maps of states (usually free from state's tourism department)
- razor
- roll of toilet tissue
- gloves (warm)
- toothbrush and paste
- floss
- down or wool socks
- laundry bag
- tent and ground cloth
- turtlenecks
- hammer (10-oz.)
- diaper pins
- sponge
- small pillow cover (can be stuffed with clothes or plastic inflatable pillow)
- sleeping bag and liner bag
- air mattress (lightweight plastic)

- handkerchief
- sunglasses
- Gatorade powder and scoop
- backup pair of prescription glasses or contact lenses (if you wear them)
- aspirin
- money belt (to hold bulk of your money, identification, credit cards, etc.), especially if riding solo or in a small party.

Pit stop.

Chapter Two

Tips for Training and Safety

TRAINING

There are two types of training I recommend for this undertaking—mental and physical. The background reading you do before starting your adventure will pay great rewards later. Read about the trail as much as possible, both fiction and nonfiction. Using the bibliography at the back of this book as your starting point, let your imagination be your guide. You might want to join the Santa Fe Trail Association, also listed in the appendix. The group's newsletter *Wagon Tracks* is full of interesting tidbits that you cannot get from books, and the articles are bound to get you in the mood for your trip into the past. Although delving into trail lore is optional, I recommend it highly, as it will enhance your enjoyment as you visit forts, Santa Fe Trail ruts, and historic towns.

Physical training, however, is *not* optional. The full-length trip should not be undertaken without at least three months' bicycling preparation. If you are a longtime cyclist, it may be shorter; if you are new to the sport, you will want to train longer. For the novice, renting a touring bike for weekend rides will help you decide what type, make, and gear ratios work best.

One of the best ways to become a competent cyclist—and have fun doing it—is to join a bicycle club or ride group. If your town does not have one, find like-minded people and form one of your own. Team up with a local bicycle shop (if you have one), and after picking out safe and interesting routes, schedule Saturday or Sunday rides and publicize the invitation.

Learn to be your own coach. Keep a logbook with not just mileage but also notes about gearing, diet, pulse rate, and anything else that seems relevant to your training. Make sure that you check your tires before each outing, inflating them when necessary both before and during your ride.

Several factors are important if you are going to ride your best. Establish a comfortable, efficient riding position on your bike. Bike shops usually have personnel who can advise you wisely about seating position. Basically, your seat should be high enough so that when your pedals are all the way down, your knees are practically straightened out.

Though it sounds obvious, it is also important to pedal correctly—in circles, applying pressure all the way around the stroke. Use your heels to drag the pedals down. Pull back at the bottom and kick across the top. When going uphill, use the top of your foot pressed against the top of your toe-clip to pull the pedal back up. It is most comfortable, and safest, to wear biking shoes.

Within reason, the more training mileage, the better. Of course, this depends on your work schedule and other factors. If possible, try to enter a century ride (100 miles) or a half-century before you leave for your Santa Fe Trail trek. This will build confidence, strength, and ability. Bicycling magazines and books from your local bookstore or library will offer suggestions for productive and safe training schedules.

If you do not already watch your diet, now is the time to begin thinking about nutrition. Common sense rules that apply to other sports and good health in general also apply to the cyclist's diet. *Do* eat natural, organic food if possible, and consume abundant fresh fruit and vegetables. *Don't* eat fried foods; and avoid white sugar, flour, and milk with more than 4 percent fat. The less processing your food has, the better.

On the road, take healthful snacks and thirst-quenching liquid with you as well as water. It is a good idea to take a sip of liquid every ten minutes, and to eat before hunger strikes.

Stretching is an important part of training that should not be ignored. Do it religiously for at least ten minutes before every outing. You can devise your own routine, but I recommend the following:

☞ *Shoulder stretches.* Stand with your feet apart and put your arms behind your buttocks, hands clasped. Bend slowly forward, raising your arms as high as comfortably possible. Repeat this several times.

☞ *Neck-rolls.* Slowly roll your head from your right shoulder, forward, to your left shoulder and then back. Contract your back muscles, trying to flex your shoulder blades until they seem to almost touch. Repeat five times.

☞ *Toe-touches.* With your knees slightly bent, try to put your palms flat on the ground or floor. If this is easy, go for touching your wrists. Release; stand upright, and repeat. Do this five times. The more flexible you become, the less likely you are to suffer soreness or injuries on the ride.

☞ *Leg stretches.* Sit on the floor with your legs stretched out straight to the left and the right. With your arms over your head and hands clasped together, bend your waist and stretch

to the right, the center, and the left. This
should be done slowly and thoroughly. Repeat
several times.

Add your own favorite stretches to the above.

SAFETY

A longer treatise could be written about bicycling
safely, but I will make my recommendations short
and, I hope, pithy. The major rule is to *remain alert
and ride defensively.* Try to think of motorized traffic as something with which you want to harmo-
niously coexist. In any contest, the cyclist will
inevitably come out the loser, sometimes with trag-
ic results.

Riding rules which should be uppermost:

☞ Always wear good headgear. Micro-shell
helmets—Styrofoam with a thin-shell plastic
cover—are best. There are several styles to
choose from and even high-tech breeds. As
with most equipment items, it is good to talk
with other cyclists to learn what they
recommend.
☞ Keep your bicycle in top-notch operating
condition. This includes tires, brakes, gears,
seat—everything. Be prepared to make repairs
and adjustments on the road during training.
Check everything the night before, but in the
morning, check air pressure once again. Any
adjustment can be done faster and better in
camp than on a hot and weedy roadside.
☞ Never ride *against* traffic. It is not only ille-
gal: it is suicidal. Unlike runners, who should
always face oncoming traffic, you should think
of your bicycle in some ways as a car. Motor-

ists, especially those turning onto a thorough-fare, are not looking for bicycles approaching from the wrong side of the road. Remember that in most states, bicycles are classed as vehicles subject to essentially similar rules as motor vehicles. Should you ever find yourself involved in an accident, your status in any court will be improved if you were riding legally.

☞ Constantly scan the road behind. While I highly recommend a rearview mirror—either the kind that attaches to your helmet or to your handlebar—in heavy traffic, the mirror alone is not enough. Practice looking over

Preparing to leave from the Santa Fe plaza, New Mexico.

your left and right shoulders so you can do this without losing your balance.

☞ In towns, try to ride in a straight line, a car door's width away from any parked vehicles you encounter. When no cars are in a parking lane, position your bike just to the right of the traffic lane. Do not ride along the curb.

☞ Use hand signals to tell motorists what you intend to do. Cyclists should use the same hand signals as motorists.

☞ Be predictable when cycling in traffic. Avoid sudden maneuvers that might throw off vehicle drivers.

☞ Practice riding in a straight line. Wobbling from left to right is never safe in traffic (or anywhere else).

☞ Even if you know you have the right-of-way, never contest it with a motorist. An experienced cyclist suggested the following warning as something to keep in mind:

> Here lies the body of Biker Grey,
> struck while contesting the right-of-way.
> He was right, dead right, as he rode along.
> But he's just as dead as if he'd been wrong!

☞ Stay alert. Do not try to take pictures except during rest stops, and leave your portable stereo in your pannier for nights at the campsite. Concentrate and be aware of situations as they change around you. Your ears can warn of danger even if you do not see it.

☞ Watch for glass, gravel, gratings of all kinds (from sewage drains to railroad crossings to cattle guards). Warn others behind you by a hand gesture and a one-word admonition ("Gravel!," "Glass!," and so forth).

New Mexico to Colorado

*Wall, kiva, and church, Pecos National Monument,
New Mexico.*

Doorway detail, Pecos National Monument, New Mexico.

Chapter Three

New Mexico
Santa Fe to Las Vegas

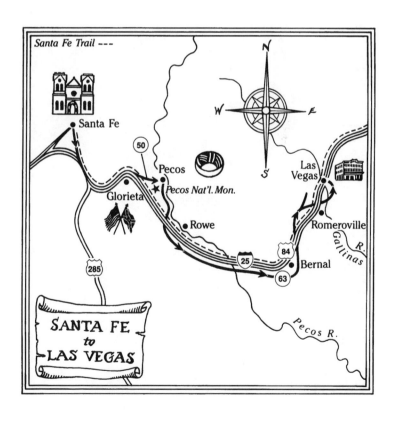

Vigas and adobe, Pecos National Monument, New Mexico.

DAY 1 / 72 miles, 115 km

HIGHLIGHTS:
- ⌐ Santa Fe Plaza
- ⌐ Battle of Glorieta Pass—Civil War Site
- ⌐ Pecos National Monument
- ⌐ Old Town Plaza, Las Vegas

Today's course, moderate and gently hilly, will dip south and northeastward. Before you leave Santa Fe, be sure to spend some time exploring the **Santa Fe Plaza**. For the first Santa Fe Trail adventurers, this was the destination. After the trail was established, wagon train traffic constantly flowed east- and westward. For those who start the trek in Santa Fe, this is the beginning.

If you are able to arrive in Santa Fe a day or two early, make sure to include a visit to the Palace of the Governors. Dating back to 1610, it is as old as the city itself. Seat of the Spanish government that reigned for many decades, occupied by Indians for thirteen years, the Palace of the Governors today is a repository of New Mexican history and art. Also visit the Fine Arts Museum, noteworthy for its fine auditorium and art collection. Last but not least, take special notice of the stone plaque near the southeast corner of the plaza marking the end of the Santa Fe Trail.

After a final check of gear and bidding farewell to any friends and loved ones who may be on hand for your historic leave-taking, mount up and begin the biking adventure of a lifetime! Leaving the plaza, walk your bike on Old Santa Fe Trail past La Fonda Hotel. (This block is one-way going into the plaza.) At the end of the one-way block on Water Street, mount up. Take a left on Water Street, then an immediate right on Old Santa Fe Trail.

Heading out from the plaza, you will pass three historic churches, all on your left: St. Francis Cathedral, a towering Romanesque structure built by Archbishop Jean Baptiste Lamy; Loretto Chapel, with its winding "miraculous staircase" (it was built without nails or visible means of support); and San Miguel Chapel, reputedly the country's oldest church.

Santa Fe has many charms, but courtesy to cyclists is not one of them, so watch very carefully as you pedal out of town. After the plaza, Santa Fe Trail is narrow and heavily traveled, so you will want to use your rearview mirror and avoid weaving. If you are with others, now is a good time to ride single file ("drafting"). At the corner of Old Santa Fe Trail and Paseo de Peralta, about ½ mile along your way, note The Roundhouse, New Mexico's capitol building, designed after the Pueblo Indian Zia symbol and recently remodeled. The road narrows beyond this intersection, and for a bit less than a mile you will be pedaling gradually uphill. You will come to a Y, which indicates that Santa Fe Trail veers off to the left. Go *right* on Old Pecos Trail. *Do not angle left* on Old Santa Fe Trail.

Do not worry about road signs at this point: stay on Old Pecos Trail, and travel east about 3½ miles to a traffic light at the juncture of Pecos Trail and Rodeo Road. At this point, turn left to get on the frontage road, Old Las Vegas Highway. Exercise extreme caution at the intersection: even though there is a traffic light, it may be necessary to walk your bike across the Old Pecos Trail to the Old Las Vegas Highway.

Mildly hilly terrain and lovely views of the Sangre de Cristo foothills make this stretch enjoyable, but the narrowness of the road requires vigilance. Take the frontage road. After going 9.8 miles, you will come to the lovely red-roofed Cañoncito adobe church, which is a good resting spot. After a break, proceed under the overpass and turn right onto I-25. Watch carefully for traffic. The gentle piñon-covered hills and interesting rock formations on either side of the road will not offer a distraction so much as an accompaniment. After traveling 5 miles on the interstate on some fairly steep terrain, take Exit 299. At the top, turn left. Signs will announce the Glorieta Baptist Assembly, which will be off to your extreme left. A road sign at Highway 50 points toward Pecos: take a right turn. Shortly after the turn is a historic marker commemorating the Civil War's **Battle of Glorieta Pass** on March 28, 1862, during which Union troops destroyed all Confederacy hopes for taking New Mexico; while the Confederates won the battle, the Union troops captured all their supplies and ammunition, thus halting the southern campaign.

The road along this stretch, though not usually very busy, is patchy and occasionally dangerous. There is lovely countryside here, with an interesting assortment of cabins, countryside homes, auto repair shops, and souvenir stands.

After you see the "Welcome to Pecos" sign, cross into San Miguel County and then wind your way onto the main road of Pecos. Once you come to the main road, take a right turn on Highway 63 and travel east out of town toward the **Pecos National Monument**. On your left and right, note the lovely ranch land donated to the monument by actress-philanthropist Greer Garson Fogelson. Look for the blue lightning bolts on the pink stuccoed walls, an emblem of the ranch. The monument, administered by the National Park Service, is worthy of a visit.

The Pecos ruins date back to A.D. 1100, when Anasazi farmers moved eastward from the Rio Grande. Then known by its Indian name Cicuyé, Pecos Pueblo was originally five stories high and housed twenty-five hundred people. In 1541, Spanish *conquistadores* under the command of Francisco Vásquez de Coronado passed through in their fruitless search for the treasures of the supposed

Seven Cities of Cíbola. By the early 1600s, as Spanish priests tried to Christianize the Indians, the Misión de Nuestra Señora de los Angeles de Porciúncula had been built.

Even in its present dilapidated state, the church is impressive: its adobe walls are seven feet thick; the roof timbers weigh several tons. Fortresslike, it must have been an effective reminder to the Indians of the invincibility of the Catholic Church. The mission walls served later as a landmark for travelers on the Santa Fe Trail.

Attached to the church is the *convento*, a rambling communal dwelling where priests carried on the mission's daily life. Within the convento walls is a kiva built after the Pueblo revolt of 1680—symbol of the Indians' desire to go back to their traditional ways.

From 1915 to 1927, Pecos was excavated. It was one of the first southwestern ruins to be researched, and work done here by American archeologist Alfred V. Kidder led to a classification system used for sites throughout the Southwest.

The visitor center houses a museum with a fine pottery collection, a theater featuring an informative film about the ruins, and a bookstore. The film, narrated by Greer Garson Fogelson, is an excellent combination of factual material and imagination. Admission to the 1¼-mile walk around the ruins is minimal, and the walk gives one the real flavor of the life of the pueblo's ancient residents. Try to stretch your schedule to include it.

Taking your leave of Pecos National Monument, return to Highway 63, take a right, and continue 6 miles south till you reach I-25, which is also Highway 84. There is a frontage road to the right of northbound I-25 that will take you the remaining 38 miles to Las Vegas. The advantage of frontage roads is that they are less heavily trafficked, but the disadvantage is that they are usually rougher and more flat-tire producing than the highways that parallel them. On the pastoral stretch from Rowe, you will pass through the small towns of San Jose, Bernal, and Romeroville.

When you reach Las Vegas, exit Highway 85 at New Mexico Avenue until you reach National Avenue. Take a right on National Avenue and follow it into the historic **Old Town Plaza**. Even if you are not staying at the Plaza Hotel, this is a good place to pause and get your bearings. An alternative place to spend the night is Highlands University (see appendix in order to make advance plans to camp or stay in the dormitories).

It was in Las Vegas that General Stephen Watts Kearny and the Army of the West came on August 15, 1846, to claim Nuevo Mexico territory from the Mexican government. The town's character changed from sleepy to bustling during later trail days: approximately five thousand wagons passed through in 1866.

With the arrival of the Atchison, Topeka, and Santa Fe (AT&SF) Railway in 1879, Las Vegas grew busier—and noisier—thanks to the exploits of outlaws and desperados such as Doc Holliday, Hoodoo Brown, Dave Rudabaugh, and Billy the Kid.

If you are not too weary at the end of the day's journey, a biking tour of Las Vegas itself is highly recommended. Begin in the town's historic Carnegie Park Historic District, located directly east of the plaza. The architecture in this section varies from Queen Anne to Italianate to Victorian eclectic, and it contrasts sharply with the southwestern style around the plaza. The Carnegie District was built quite rapidly after the arrival of the AT&SF Railway. As you bike around, you will notice that the streets are laid out in orderly grid fashion. Adding to the area's charm are Lincoln and Carnegie parks, located south and north of Douglas Avenue.

As you pedal through east Las Vegas, watch especially for the stately Carnegie Library, modeled after Thomas Jefferson's home, Monticello; the English-looking Stephen B. Davis House, with its yellow stuccoed walls at the corner of Fifth and Columbia streets; and the cottage at 512 Columbia Avenue with its graceful front bay window and folk spindlework. There are at least ten other historic homes and commercial buildings in this area. See as many as time allows.

Also post-Santa Fe Trail, the Railroad Avenue area of Las Vegas merits a sightseeing tour. Comprised of hotels, busy mercantile houses, saloons and dance halls, Railroad Avenue in its heyday was a prosperous, lively thoroughfare. Its Victorian commercial buildings, the Renaissance Revival-style Gross Kelly Building, La Castañeda (an early Harvey House), and the metal-fronted Rawlins Building are all noteworthy.

The Gross Kelly Building, designed in 1898–99 by the Rapp Brothers, was used to house one of New Mexico's leading mercantile companies. After acquiring the building in 1982, the Public Service Company of New Mexico restored the exterior masonry and interior oak woodwork, a job so extensive that the building has won numerous awards and citations.

Another landmark of the post-Santa Fe Trail era, La Castañeda Hotel, has an enchanting air of bygone elegance. The graceful facade with its arched walkway faces the railroad tracks. Park and lock your bike and take a walk though the grand lobby and dining room, both relatively intact.

Across the street from La Castañeda looms the formerly splendid Rawlins Building, residence for the Harvey girls who staffed the hotel dining room. Note especially the recessed storefronts on the first story and the Ionic columns and swag panels of the upper story.

After all this, you should be ready for a hot shower, a hearty dinner, and a good night's sleep. Tomorrow, it's on to Wagon Mound!

Cañoncito Church, Apache Canyon, New Mexico.

Wagons and walls, Fort Union, New Mexico.

Chapter Four

New Mexico
Las Vegas to Wagon Mound

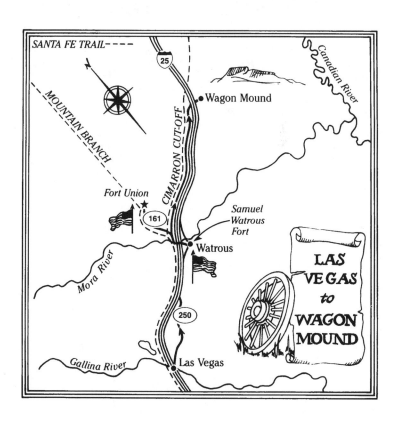

Wagon Mound, New Mexico, resembling a conestoga wagon, was a famous landmark for the pioneers on the Santa Fe Trail, ca. 1882. Photo by J.R. Riddle. Courtesy Museum of New Mexico, Neg. No. 56293.

DAY 2 / 60 miles, 96 km

HIGHLIGHTS:
- Watrous
- Fort Union National Monument

Today's moderate trek takes you from Las Vegas north to the town of Watrous, to picturesque Fort Union, and finally to Wagon Mound (formerly the Mexican settlement of Santa Clara). You will want to allow several hours for Fort Union National Monument and also take time to enjoy the vistas surrounding this historic site. As Marc Simmons points out in *Following the Santa Fe Trail,* "The approach to the fort and the site itself offer superlative views of a landscape that has experienced only minor changes since the days of wagon caravans."

But on to today's journey. Leave Las Vegas via Ninth Street north to Mills Avenue. When you reach the junction of Mills Avenue and Highway 85, turn left. Continue on Highway 85 until it goes right. At this point, you will bike under I-25 to Frontage Road 250 on the right side of I-25.

When Frontage Road 250 ends, take a left, then a right on I-25. You have the option of taking the frontage road on the right of I-25 or the interstate itself. The disadvantage to the frontage road is an inferior surface; the drawback to the interstate is heavier traffic. If you do choose to brave the traffic, however, the shoulders are wide and relatively smooth.

After about 20 miles on either I-25 or the frontage road, take the turnoff marked "Watrous." About 3/4 of a mile from the I-25 interchange is the pitched-roof white building that serves as the Doolittle Ranch headquarters. **Watrous** was named after Samuel B. Watrous, who arrived in the area in 1849 and traded with Santa Fe Trail travelers. In *Following the Santa Fe Trail*, Simmons notes that one

Watrous daughter married William Tipton, who had a nearby town named after him, and another Watrous daughter married Sapello stage station manager George Gregg. The mysterious deaths in the mid-1880s of Watrous and his son were probably a case of murder.

After viewing Watrous, bicycle through on Highway 161. The road goes left and over I-25. Once you go through the interchange, you will still be on Highway 161, which will take you to Fort Union in about 8 miles. Enjoy the wide-open spaces: there is a good chance of seeing herds of antelope grazing on the plains. Take advantage of the peace and quiet. As you pedal back in time, let your imagination flow freely.

The gently uphill, rolling road to Fort Union offers splendid views. As Marc Simmons points out in *Following the Santa Fe Trail,* the landscape "has experienced only minor changes since the days of the wagon caravans." Simmons recommends several hours for a tour of **Fort Union National Monument**.

Only stark ruins remain today, but Fort Union was once an extensive installation that included a military post and related structures, as well as a separate quartermaster depot with warehouses, corrals, shops, offices and sleeping quarters.

The excellent visitor center and museum is the place to begin exploring Fort Union. A self-guided tour around the parade grounds and ruins conveys much information through audio speakers and interpretive signs.

There were three Fort Unions, all built in this vicinity. The site was established for defense in the summer of 1851 by Lieutenant Colonel Edwin V. Sumner. Santa Fe had been condemned as military department headquarters because of its alleged "vice and corruption." The soldiers posted at Fort Union were to protect the trail's western end from Indian raids and stagecoach attacks.

Fort Union also served as a depository for military supplies to be dispersed to installations throughout the southwestern frontier.

A few ruins of the first Fort Union can be seen about a mile to the west of the monument. You can spot them at the bottom of a long, wooded ridge. Pending permission from monument headquarters, you can also walk on a ranch road to the site. The second Fort Union, known as the "Star Fort," was constructed during the Civil War but never saw action. It was abandoned in 1863 and is marked on the walking tour. The third Fort Union was begun the same year as the Star Fort closed down. Its adobe and stone remains are the main attraction of the monument.

In 1879 the railroad came to Watrous, diminishing the fort's significance. Fort Union ceased operation in 1891. Special events and costumed reenactments happen during the summer. Check the appendix to write ahead for the current schedule.

Leaving Fort Union, retrace your route back on Highway 161 to the frontage road on the left side of I-25. Take this road all the way into Wagon Mound.

As you approach Wagon Mound, look to the right of the frontage road and I-25 for the loaf-shaped silhouette of the mountain. It served as a milestone for travelers going out from the East or returning from the West on the trail. At first travelers referred to the mountain as a high-topped shoe; later it became popular to compare it with a covered wagon pulled by oxen; you can decide for yourself which description fits better. Either way, it was a famous landmark during trail days.

The town of Wagon Mound is nestled at the base of the mountain. Look for the exit sign marked "Wagon Mound" and pedal on in. The town has a trailer park with several campsites where tents can be pitched. Water and restrooms are available, but no shower facilities. (See appendix for more information.)

On the road.

Chapter Five

New Mexico
Wagon Mound to Cimarron

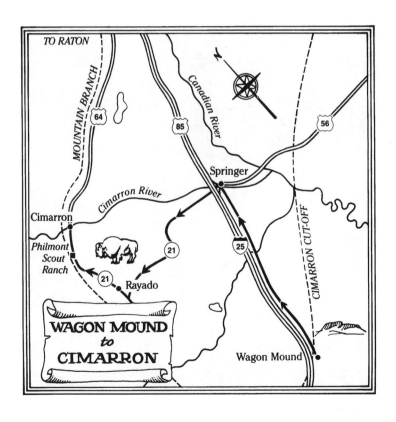

Old Mill Museum, Cimarron, New Mexico.

DAY 3 / 57 miles, 91 km

HIGHLIGHTS:
- ⁓ Philmont Scout Ranch
- ⁓ Villa Philmonte
- ⁓ Aztec Flour Mill Museum
- ⁓ St. James Hotel (formerly Don Diego Tavern)

Today's pleasant, moderate ride will give you the flavor of northern New Mexico and take you to Cimarron, one of the most important stops for wagon and coach traffic on the Mountain Branch of the Santa Fe Trail.

Leave Wagon Mound via the frontage road on the right side of I-25 and pedal 25 miles into the small town of Springer, New Mexico. The crossing of U.S. 85 and U.S. 56 in this town represents the modern convergence of the Mountain Branch and the Cimarron Cut-off of the trail. (Northeast of Las Vegas, New Mexico, near Watrous, the Santa Fe Trail divides into the Mountain Branch, north, and the southerly Cimarron Cut-off. The latter saved ten days and was used for 75 percent of trade. It was nearly waterless, however, and much harder on travelers and livestock. ~~The actual historical convergence is found in La Junta, Colorado.)~~ delete

You will probably hit Springer around lunchtime. For a bit of local color, you might want to try the cafe on the town's main street. When I was there, it was called "Stockman's Cafe" and was filled with interesting local folks, including the editor of The *Springer News Bulletin*, the town's biweekly newspaper. You will find the people to be friendly, and they also can be helpful. One of the pleasures of traveling by bike rather than car is that people along the way often seem more eager to strike up a conversation with bicyclists than motorists.

After having lunch in Springer, take Highway 21 for the remaining 34 miles to Cimarron. With its rolling hills and lovely vistas, this stretch of road should allow you to make very good time. The next milestone on your route will be Rayado, a town established in 1848 by trader, trapper, and land baron Lucien B. Maxwell and others. Because it had a water supply fed by snow runoff from surrounding mountains, Rayado was well suited for cattle and farming. It was also the home and farming place of Kit Carson for a short time. A small military post was built here in 1850 to provide Santa Fe Trail travelers protection between Raton Pass and Las Vegas. During the summer months, in a building that is a reconstruction of Kit Carson's house, the **Philmont Scout Ranch** operates a museum. A Daughters of the American Revolution (DAR) marker is posted in front of the building. If the museum is open, take time to visit. Note especially the covered wagon reputedly used by French trader Ceran St. Vrain.

Continue on Highway 21 to reach **Villa Philmonte**, the mansion of oilman Waite Phillips, who from 1930 to 1940 donated the surrounding land for the Philmont Scout Ranch, which today serves as a prized camping destination for scouts from all over the country. Special camping expeditions and rigorous wilderness adventures are scheduled throughout the summer.

After your tour of Villa Philmonte, cycle out the tree-lined driveway to Highway 21 and continue on toward Cimarron. Good road surface, little traffic, and green, rolling hills make for a pleasant ride. Look for buffalo herds that roam these fields. Maintained by the scout ranch, some of these beasts are offered up each summer for the scouts' annual buffalo roast.

Cimarron, an important stopping point on the Mountain Branch of the Santa Fe Trail, is worthy of a tour. It served as headquarters for the Lucien B. Maxwell land grant, some 1,700,000 acres that

Maxwell acquired in 1864 as the result of his marriage to the daughter of Carlos Beaubien.

Maxwell's home was famous for a time as the Santa Fe Trail's first civilized stop for westbound travelers. However, true to the fickleness of Old West fame and fortune, by 1870 Maxwell had lost both wealth and prestige. It seems that the cause of his downfall was bad mining ventures, a common leveler of the times. Until Maxwell's downfall, his empire served as an outfitting center for prospectors, trappers, and hunters who were headed for the mountains.

The present-day town is divided by the Cimarron River into the old and new sections, conveniently separating the historic section from the modern section; bicycling from Philmont will bring you first to the latter. Before establishing camp or checking into a hotel for the night, take a couple hours for a closer look at this Old West town. A good beginning point is the **Aztec Flour Mill**, built by Maxwell in 1864 and now a museum operated by the Cimarron Historical Society.

Also pay a brief visit to the 100-year-old **St. James Hotel**, a colorful Victorian style establishment where Jesse James allegedly stayed. The building has the reputation for being haunted, and recently the St. James has staged monthly "murder mystery weekends." Call ahead for the schedule (see appendix). The first floor rooms, elegantly appointed and named after denizens of the frontier, are open for viewing. There is a restaurant serving breakfast, lunch, and dinner.

Raton Pass, New Mexico to Colorado.

Chapter Six

New Mexico & Colorado
Cimarron to Trinidad

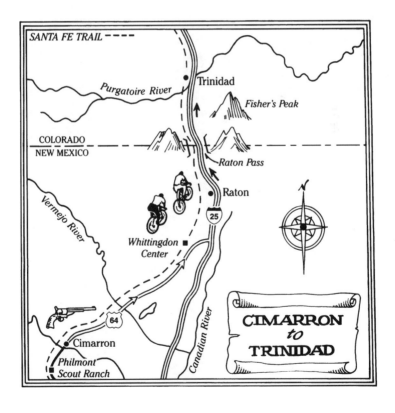

Pioneer Museum, Trinidad, Colorado.

DAYS 4 and 5 / 69 miles, 110 km
(LAYOVER DAY)

HIGHLIGHTS:
- ⇀ Whittingdon Center
- ⇀ Raton Pass
- ⇀ Don Felipe Baca House
- ⇀ Pioneer Museum
- ⇀ Bloom House
- ⇀ Aultman Museum of Photography
- ⇀ Louden-Henritze Archaeology Museum
- ⇀ Mountain Park Loop (side trip)
- ⇀ Cucharas Pass (side trip)

Today's moderate-to-difficult trek is steeped in history and scenic beauty. It includes the 6-mile climb up Raton Pass, the passage from New Mexico into Colorado, and a chance to spend your well-earned day off in one of Colorado's loveliest towns.

Leaving Cimarron a few blocks beyond the St. James Hotel, you will come to an intersection with Highway 64 to Raton. Continue on Highway 64 about 31 miles to the turnoff for the **Whittingdon Center**. Founded in 1973 by the National Rifle Association (NRA) to provide optimal facilities for its marksmanship, hunting, and gun-safety programs, the center ranges over fifty square miles of rolling foothills.

Depending on your inclination, you might want to visit the Whittingdon's new administration center. To get there, turn left off Route 64 and pedal a short distance over a packed dirt road. After obtaining permission from the personnel on duty, bicycle or lock your bike and walk 1 mile out the dirt road for the main attraction here: a splendid view of Santa Fe Trail ruts, announced by a large sign. (Unless you have unusually tough tires, it would probably be best to lock up your bike and walk.)

After viewing the ruts, return to Highway 64 and turn left (northeast) toward Raton. In 4 miles, you will reach a junction with I-25. Bike carefully into the interstate, staying well to the right of the white borderline, and continue on to Raton, leaving on Exit 451 (Clayton Road). Take a left on Clayton to Second Street (Highways 85 and 87).

Take a right on Second Street and proceed through town carefully. Depending on the time of day, traffic can be heavy. (When I passed through on the first Santa Fe Trail Bicycle Trek in 1990, our entourage entered Raton during the noon hour, was greeted by the president of the chamber of commerce, and traveled through town with a police escort!)

The street you are on, Second, turns into Canyon Drive (Highways 85 and 87, once again), which becomes I-25 up and over **Raton Pass**. For this daunting 6-mile uphill haul, you should begin by gearing down and finding a comfortable, sustainable pace. On the bright side, there is plenty of shoulder for most of the pass. Remember, however, that just as you are struggling with the grade, so are trucks and trailers that will be passing you. As you concentrate on your own ascent, be extra mindful of traffic. The air grows thinner, and the climb may seem endless. You will pass a "Welcome to Colorado" sign and cross over the land where Richens Lacy "Uncle Dick" Wootton, a mountain man and Indian scout, operated a tollgate in the mid-1860s.

"Uncle Dick," recognizing a chance for profit, capitalized on the difficulty of this stretch of terrain. Although the pass had been used for hundreds of years by Indians and explorers, it was too rugged for Conestoga wagons. In true entrepreneurial fashion, "Uncle Dick" carved a gentler passage through the mountains and stationed a tollgate for everyone who came by.

As you wend your way up the last curve of Raton Pass, you might contemplate the fate of those early Santa Fe Trail travelers who balked at paying "Uncle Dick's" tollgate fare. Their only alternative was to turn around the oxen team and travel a 100-mile detour to the east! No detours are possible for the cyclist going over the pass, but just when you think you cannot face another rising grade, you're at the crest!

After a glorious moment or so of pausing to admire the view, you can relax going downhill all the way to Trinidad, approximately 11 miles. First, however, be sure to check your brakes and cables and adjust your rearview mirror. And once again, you need to be aware of traffic alongside and behind you. Losing control on the pass's rapidly descending curves is all too easy—for bikes and trucks and cars. After the exhilaration of conquering the summit, you may find yourself in a "no-holds-barred" frame of mind. Resist the impulse to "zoom": keep safety foremost.

The views coming into Trinidad are breathtaking. Enjoy them, but do not overlook Exit 11, for this takes you off I-25 and into the Trinidad Lake area, tonight's recommended campground (see appendix).

You will come to a frontage road going south, which you'll follow until you reach the Trinidad State Recreation Area. An alternative is to stay at a motel in town, and you may prefer that after four nonstop days of cycling. If this is your choice, take Exit 13A, which will bring you to several reasonably priced motels.

After setting up camp or checking into a motel, set out for your exploration of Trinidad. There is so much to see that you will want to use whatever is left of your cycling day and the entire next day to explore.

At the top of your list should be the Don Felipe Baca House, the Bloom House, and the Pioneer Museum, must-see attractions that are all located on Main Street. By the way, Main Street follows the actual route of the Santa Fe Trail.

On the corner of Chestnut and Main stands the **Don Felipe Baca House**, built by Santa Fe Trail merchant John S. Hough in 1870 and purchased by Maria Baca in 1873. The two-story Territorial-style home is decorated inside with whitewashed walls, Spanish textiles, upholstered furniture, and religious objects, typical for a prosperous mid-Victorian, Spanish-American family of the time. The interior, with its homey touches such as a laptop writing desk and samplers of "hair art," give one a feeling for the family life of the Bacas. (Women of the time saved cuttings of their children's, husbands' or sweethearts' hair and wove them into fanciful wreaths or "flowers.")

As Marc Simmons notes in *On the Santa Fe Trail,* rancher Don Felipe Baca was "the principal founder of Trinidad." In the early 1860s, he and his family settled along the Purgatoire River. Baca, a farmer, merchandiser, cattle- and sheep-rancher, was one of the town's most prominent citizens. He was president of the school board and a representative to the territorial legislature.

Behind the Baca House is an adobe building that once served as the servants' quarters and is now the **Pioneer Museum**. A visit there will give you glimpses of the prominent people in Trinidad's history. In the museum courtyard, you will find buggies and freight wagons used to transport people and goods along the Santa Fe Trail.

Next door to the Baca House is the **Bloom House**, the mansion of another prominent early Trinidad family. Frank G. Bloom came to the city in 1867. Bloom was the store manager, one of the town's first bankers, and director of the Bloom Cattle Company. His home is decorated elegantly with patterned carpets, varied wallpapers, lace curtains and a fine collection of Victorian silver and china.

Other attractions near the heart of Trinidad include the **Aultman Museum of Photography**, a visual record of early-day Trinidad taken by O. E. Aultman and his son Glenn, and the **Louden-Henritze Archaeology Museum**, which includes a look at millions of years of southwest Colorado's geological history. In this small but interesting museum, you will see not only dioramas that show geology of the area, but also plant and marine fossils and artifacts of Trinidad's prehistoric inhabitants.

....

SUGGESTED SIDE TRIPS

If you have the time and inclination, a beautiful and rewarding side trip is the **Monument Park Loop**. Take State Road 12 west from Trinidad and bike 35 miles through the North Fork River valley to 1,200-acre Monument Park. Be sure to pack food, for although you will go through small towns every 5 to 10 miles, there is not much available to purchase.

For a two-day side trip, you might want to bicycle an additional 18 miles on to the strikingly beautiful 9,941-foot **Cucharas Pass** (in San Isabel National Forest). Camp there overnight, and the next day bicycle through La Veta to join U.S. 160 at Walsenburg.

Bloom House, Trinidad, Colorado.

SECTION THREE

Colorado to Kansas

Limestone schoolhouse outside Lamar, Colorado.

Santa Fe steam engine, Lamar, Colorado.

Chapter Seven

Colorado
Trinidad to La Junta

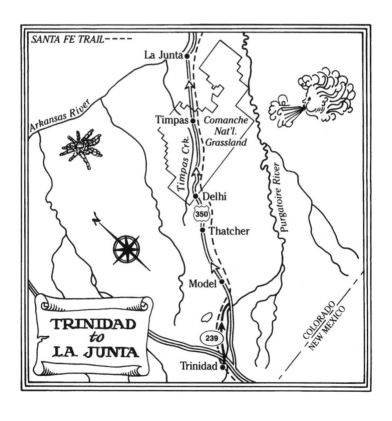

Koshare Indian Museum, La Junta, Colorado.

DAY 6 / 87 miles, 139 km

HIGHLIGHTS:
- ~ Comanche Grassland National Preserve
- ~ Koshare Indian Museum

Today's long, long journey is in many ways a peaceful one: beautiful country roads, somber ghost towns, the scenic Comanche grasslands; and at the end, there is a gem of a museum at La Junta's Otero Junior College. After a rest stop in Trinidad, and a week of cycling, you should be prepared to tackle this day of the trek, which is just short of a "century" ride. The countryside is lonely but picturesque, and in many ways it looks (and probably feels) much as it did during Santa Fe Trail days.

It would be well to pack a lunch before leaving Trinidad. When I bicycled this stretch, there were neither gas stations nor grocery stores. Things may have changed, but why take a chance?

Leave town on Goddard Avenue, which can be reached easily from Main Street. Several blocks beyond the Bloom and Baca Houses, take a left turn from Main onto Linden Avenue, cross the Purgatoire River and the railroad tracks and then turn right on Goddard Avenue. Goddard will take you to Highway 239. (This path out of town follows the original Santa Fe Trail.) Take a left onto I-25 entrance to reach Highway 239 (which will veer off to the right). Look for signs to the towns of El Moro and Hoehne. Highway 239 is a beautiful country road: take time to look into the barnyards and read the names on mailboxes. It will end at El Moro, at which point you will encounter a "239 Ends" sign. Go right at first intersection past "239 Ends" sign to Hoehne. Stay on the pavement to Hoehne, going *straight* at all intersections. In about two miles, you will reach Highway 350.

Seven miles beyond the junction of Highways 239 and 350, you will pass through the town of Model—which has a store that sells food and drinks—and beyond that, Tyrone and Thatcher. When you reach the latter, you will be halfway to La Junta. It is a good place to stop, rest, and have a picnic lunch. When I cycled with a group, we discovered the stone ruins of a burned-down house in Thatcher, found convenient seats, and lunched viewing the terrain from our own private Pompeii.

A long stretch looms ahead. Now would be an excellent time to check your seat height, put air in your tires if they need it, apply sunscreen or add a windbreaker, drink water, and do a few limbering-up exercises. After your Thatcher pause, push onward to La Junta.

As you near the **Comanche Grassland National Preserve**, look for tarantulas crossing the road. Seriously! When I bicycled this terrain, we saw a goodly number of the hairy critters skittering nimbly across the highway. Besides, after leaving Thatcher there is not much to do in the flat, open countryside besides look for tarantulas and try to make good time. The next town after Thatcher is Delhi, seemingly but perhaps not really deserted.

Running to your west is Timpas Creek, a source of brackish water for earlier trail travelers. Army of the West marchers described how thirst-craved men would compete with their beasts for a drink. It was a race for the men to drink the water first, before the horses and oxen befouled it.

When you reach the La Junta city limits, look for Tenth Street, your signal to leave Highway 350. Take a right onto Tenth and cycle to Colorado Avenue. At Colorado Avenue, take another right to reach Otero Junior College, where you will want to visit the **Koshare Indian Museum** at 115 West Eighteenth Street, at the corner of Santa Fe Avenue.

The museum is the home of the Koshare Indian dancers, a scouting troop with a national reputation for their productions. Few, if any, of the Boy Scouts in the Koshare troupe are Native Americans, but the dances in their repertoire are authentic representations of traditional Indian dances.

The Koshares give approximately fifty performances a year at home and at various conventions throughout the area. Money from these performances was used to build the museum, which houses an impressive collection of authentic Plains Indians artifacts—basketry, beadwork, and jewelry—many dating back to Santa Fe Trail times. The Koshare Indian Museum is open daily except for Thanksgiving, Christmas, and New Year's Day. The spacious Kiva serves as a hostelry for thousands of scouts who travel through each year. Dances are presented from mid-June through early August. For show times, call or write the Koshare Indian Museum (see appendix).

Friendly horses, Comanche Grassland National Preserve, Colorado.

Chapter Eight

Colorado
La Junta to Lamar

Bent's Old Fort, east of La Junta, Colorado.

DAY 7 / 69 miles, 110 km

HIGHLIGHTS:
- Bent's Old Fort
- Fort Lyon
- Bent's New Fort
- Big Timbers Museum

Leave La Junta on Highway 109 to 194, a pleasant road that begins today's trek on a pastoral note. Look for "loaf of bread" haystacks, prairie dog fields, and both deserted and inhabited farmhouses.

In 6 miles you will reach **Bent's Old Fort**, a national historical site and one of the most important landmarks on the Santa Fe Trail. Built by brothers Charles and William Bent, the fort was an important frontier connection point. From the mud-and-straw citadel, American trade radiated south to Mexico, west toward the Pacific, and north to southern Wyoming. Bent's fort, originally built in 1833–34 and destroyed in 1849, was reconstructed in the mid-1970s by the National Park Service. Its storerooms, shops, and living quarters all have period furnishings. Of special interest is the room where nineteen-year-old diarist Susan Magoffin spent nearly two weeks.

Along with the Bent brothers, Ceran St. Vrain was part of a very profitable trading company. All three men hailed from St. Louis, lured west by the fur trade of the Upper Missouri. They were armed with some capital and experience, but the real secret of their success was their friendly relations with the Mexicans and Indians—Cheyenne, Arapaho, Comanche, Kiowa, Prairie Apache, and Pawnee. They managed, almost miraculously, to create an atmosphere of peace conducive to good trading.

Bent's fort was a mecca for trappers and mountain men. After bringing in their furs, they would usually stay to gamble, spin yarns, and carouse. Men who worked and played at the post included Lucien B. Maxwell, Thomas Boggs, Baptiste Charbonneau, Kit Carson, and "Uncle Dick" Wootton.

In addition to its importance for trading and shelter, Bent's fort was relied on by travelers for repairs. While caravan members relaxed, post carpenters and blacksmiths could fix whatever had been damaged by the trail's harsh conditions. Oxen and mules could get a long overdue rest. Special guests were even treated to mint juleps prepared by the fort's proprietors.

The gold rush, Mexican War, and influx of adventurers and settlers helped bring about the end of profitable trading. The arrival of the hordes fouled watering spots, frightened away buffalo, and depleted the precious natural wood supply. When Charles Bent, who had been the peacekeeper with the Indians, was killed in the Taos revolt in 1847, the Bent empire collapsed. William Bent bought St. Vrain's interest in the fort, but abandoned it in 1849.

In 1954 Bent's fort was excavated by Trinidad Junior College. There has been a sustained effort since then to preserve the site. You will note DAR markers to the left of the entrance gate and by the parking lot.

Inside the fort, you can wander around the refurbished living quarters, shops, and storerooms. During the summer, costumed guides give demonstrations and dramatic interpretations. There is a well-supplied gift shop with Santa Fe Trail books, postcards, and the like.

Leaving Bent's Old Fort, continue on Highway 194 as it turns left (north) and then right (east) and finally joins Highway 50 just north of Las Animas.

Continue on Highway 50 toward **Fort Lyon**, which is currently a VA hospital. If you would like to take a side trip to the monument and ruins of **Bent's New Fort**, look for County Road 35 which turns south (right) off Highway 50. This will be 1 mile before you reach the Prowers County Line. Go south 1 mile on Bent County Road 35 to Road JJ. At this juncture, turn east (left) for ⅛ mile to a county road marked with a barely legible sign reading "R–25." Go right (south). At ¼ mile you will see the monument 150 yards to the right. Go another 100 yards, leave your bike locked, by the gate, and walk uphill to phone lines and the monument (on private land). Fort Lyon, originally named Fort Wise, guarded the eastern Colorado portion of the Santa Fe Trail.

As you head toward Lamar, some 35 miles after Bent's Old Fort, you will enter an area known during trail days as "Big Timbers."

The "timbers" were massive cottonwood and willow trees that flanked both sides of the Arkansas River. The wooded area made Big Timbers a favorite camping spot of the southern Plains Indians. The relatively lush area provided game, shelter, and firewood for the Indians, as well as feed for ponies and buffalo.

Dating as far back as Zebulon M. Pike's exploration of the southern Louisiana Purchase in 1806, Big Timbers was a haven for Santa Fe Trail travelers. Indians hunted here. Surveyors and traders paused here to rest and trade with the Indians. In the 1860s, when the area was open for settlers, Big Timbers furnished building materials for cabins and fuel for stoves.

Just before reaching the outskirts of Lamar, you will come to **Big Timbers Museum,** established by the Prowers County Historical Society. The hours are normally afternoons from 1:30 to 4:30. Prepare to spend an hour or so, as the museum holds a treasure trove of Indian and pioneer possessions. Note in particular the museum's tools and equipment, a collection that includes harnesses, plows, an oxen yoke, sodbuster, wagon odometer, and corn sheller. Other sections include the mineral and rock collection, children's toys, display cases of Indian relics (arrowheads, war clubs, beads, stone tools, and bows and arrows), a roundup of cowboy gear (saddles, chaps, bits and bridles, and clothing), and a firearms collection. A thoughtful look at these memorabilia will give you a good feeling for what life was like during frontier days.

The women's fashions displayed go from the late 1800s to the 1930s. Several rooms are set up with typical turn-of-the-century antique furnishings. And finally, do not pass by the splendid photograph collection, which will astonish and delight. Be sure to look for the "rabbit roundup" photo, which shows early Colorado citizens with four thousand rabbits which they had slain with sticks after the creatures ate their vegetable gardens!

It is less than a mile from the Big Timbers Museum to Lamar. Though Lamar is not a big town, late afternoon traffic can be busy, so enter town carefully and proceed to your camping or hotel area.

Chapter Nine

Colorado & Kansas
Lamar to Lakin

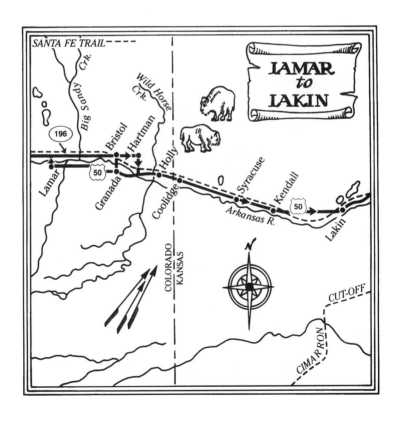

Limestone barn, Holly, Colorado.

DAY 8 / 79 miles, 126 km

HIGHLIGHTS:
- Holly Sugar Company
- Kearny County Historical Museum

Today's trek is long but rewarding: crossing the border from Colorado to Kansas is thrilling. Though the scenery pales in comparison to your first crossing (from New Mexico to Colorado), this state line seems to bring one far closer to the Santa Fe Trail spirit.

Leaving Lamar by Highway 287, pedal to the junction with Highway 196, turn right (which will be dead east) and go through Bristol to Hartman. You will then be on Highway 196, a gentle, somewhat deserted country road, for about 22 miles.

Right after you have passed through Hartman, Highway 196 jogs south, then ends. When it does, take a left onto Highway 50 and proceed east to Holly, a charming little town that deserves a thoughtful look around. With an elevation just over 3,000 feet, it is the lowest point in Colorado. The plains around Holly once sustained Cheyenne, Arapaho, Kiowa, and Comanche Indians, and vast herds of buffalo. Dominated by the Spanish and then the French, Holly and its surrounding area became part of the United States territory in 1803, less than twenty years before the Santa Fe Trail's advent. Zebulon M. Pike carried the first American flag on this route as he headed westward toward the mountains in 1806.

During trail days, Holly was known as "Pretty Camp" or "Pleasant Camp." Now a town of fewer than one thousand citizens, Holly is the site of one of the first sugar factories in Colorado. The old **Holly Sugar Company** buildings now serve as part of the office and horse barns for the Gateway Downs Race Track. In addition to being the original home of Holly Sugar, the town is headquarters of the Southeastern Colorado Co-op, a grain and farm service cooperative which has branches in surrounding Colorado and Kansas communities. The town's logo is a holly leaf, and a promotional brochure printed by the Holly Publishing Company describes the farming community as "Colorado's Christmas City."

If you brought a lunch today, the Holly City Park, right in the center of town, would be an ideal spot for a picnic. If not, there are cafes and lunchrooms. Either way, you are likely to meet some of the locals. When the first Santa Fe Trail bicycle trek of the '90s came through Holly as a group, we were greeted with signs announcing, "Welcome Santa Fe Cyclists."

A side trip well worth the extra time is to an 1860s-built barn just three blocks south of U.S. 50. Take a right (south) at the intersection of Highway 50 and Main, cross the Santa Fe Railroad tracks, and you will reach a lovely white limestone barn. Local lore has it that the square openings along the side walls were designed for guns used to fend off Indian attacks. Next to the picturesque barn is a graceful two-story stone house, also built during the Santa Fe Trail era. On the right side of the driveway, in front of a lilac bush, is a DAR marker indicating that this area was part of the trail.

Leave Holly on Highway 50, bike a mere 5 miles east, and you're in Kansas! Unless you are traveling alone, be sure to have your picture taken by the "Welcome to Kansas" sign. Also, get used to the Kansas version of Highway 50—lack of shoulder space and strong winds—as you will be on it today for another 47 miles.

The first town you will come to in Kansas is Coolidge, and then, further east, Syracuse. The latter boasts the Hamilton County Museum, which will be on your left at the town's one major intersection.

Roughly 16 miles west of Lakin, you will come to Kendall, originally named "Aubry" after the famous Santa Fe Trail distance rider Francis X. Aubry. Aubry achieved fame for his "Lightning Express," which carried freight even in winter. Apparently the post office changed the town's name to Kendall after it was discovered that another "Aubry" already existed in Kansas.

Be sure to visit the **Kearny County Historical Museum** if you reach Lakin on Tuesday, Thursday, or Sunday when the museum is open from 1 to 4 p.m.

Lakin was the end of the Mountain Branch of the Santa Fe Trail, and the historical complex consists of a museum building and annex, the White House—the oldest two-story house in Lakin—a schoolhouse, and a depot. The museum has on loan a Conestoga wagon bearing the inscription "Joseph Edgar—1831." There is a series of 1939 aerial photographs (taken by the U. S. Department of Agriculture), showing the route of the trail in the county as well as rut sites and landmarks. For additional information, contact the Director, Kearny County Museum, 101–111 S. Buffalo Street, Lakin, KS 67860; phone (316) 355-7448.

Bent's New Fort, near Lamar, Colorado.

Chapter Ten

Kansas
Lakin to Dodge City

SANTA FE TRAIL - - - -

Pawnee River

Garden City

50

Lakin

Buffalo
Game Preserve

Pierceville

Charleston

Arkansas R.

Ingalls

Cimarron
(Middle
Crossing)

Dodge City

50
56

Ft. Dodge

Ford
(Lower Crossing)

CIMARRON CUT-OFF

Cimarron River

LAKIN
to
DODGE CITY

Boot Hill Museum, Dodge City, Kansas.

DAYS 9 and 10 / 84 miles, 134 km
(LAYOVER DAY)

HIGHLIGHTS:
- Cimarron Cut-off
- Fort Dodge
- Boot Hill Museum
- Hardesty House
- Carnegie Library
- Sughrue Home
- Home of Stone
- Santa Fe Depot

Leave Lakin on U.S. Highway 50 and head northeast about 24 miles toward Garden City. Before you reach Garden City, you will come to Holcomb. For easier cycling, take the Highway 50 bypass, avoiding the city entirely. In fact, it is Highway 50 all the way.

Welcome to vast, wide-open country: big farms, big ranches. Take time to notice the expansiveness.

Wind and weather were often quite harsh to Santa Fe Trail travelers along this stretch of their route, and they can be so today. The bicycle trekkers of 1990 encountered five rainy days out of twenty-one. Other bike treks have had perfect conditions the entire time. Be prepared for sudden and extreme changes. You might wonder about the name "Garden City." It is not a misnomer, as the town is rich in gas, oil, and much-prized groundwater.

Do not let the vastness in this part of the journey oppress your spirit, and don't dismiss it as boring. To do so would be to miss a rare opportunity. In celebrating the expanse, the weather extremes, and the aloneness of the countryside, you just might recapture the spirit of the Santa Fe Trail travelers who went before.

Pierceville, to the southeast of Garden City, is a good midway spot for a roadside picnic lunch. Eat heartily, as you will soon be facing an afternoon of long, long miles. Find a grove of trees set back from the road, stretch out, and relax for a bit.

The countryside is rich in crops and cattle. Grain elevators stand out like lighthouses on the horizon. An amusing pastime is to estimate how far it is to the next towering landmark. Sometimes landmarks appear like mirages shimmering in the distance, ever receding and ephemeral. At other times, you might find your guess of a mile or two is nearly correct.

Serving as constant reminders of the Kansas beef industry are the frequent cattle feedlots, especially around Ingalls. Though not one of my favorite landmarks, they made me aware that I was definitely in the central plains. Another landmark you will want to look for is the haystack. Some are shaped like loaves of bread. Others are shaped like carpet rolls. Also look for horses, interesting barns, and buggies.

The afternoon might seem endless. This is a time for special vigilance. Watch for big rigs, semis, and farm equipment. There is usually no road shoulder at all, and you might not even be noticed by a truck driver pushing across the plains to meet a deadline and possibly blinded by a setting sun. Also use your rearview mirror to make frequent vehicle checks.

If you are riding with companions, do them the courtesy of shouting "Car back!" as soon as you spot an overtaking vehicle. If you feel a situation is dangerous, never hesitate to take preventive measures: for example, get off your bike and stand by the road to let a monstrous truck roar by. Also watch for cattle guards and free-ranging cattle, who have right-of-way on the roads. In other words, keep alert and use common sense.

While still thinking about safety, it is possible to indulge in some mental aerobics. You will grow less tired if you vary your pace with occasional speedwork. An interesting exercise is to time yourself. If you do not have an odometer on your bike, look for highway mile markers; make a mental note of the time at the beginning and end of each mile, and you will have a rough estimate of how fast you are going. Try alternating a fast and a moderate mile, or juxtapose two speedy miles with three that are slower. Not only will this help develop your pedaling speed, it will make the miles go by much more quickly.

When you pass through Cimarron, you will be at the origin of the **Cimarron Cut-off**, the preferred westbound route of some Santa Fe Trail traders. Though it was more arduous, it was about three days shorter than the Mountain Route. In fact, it (rather than the alternative) was used regularly after 1829. Up until the Mexican War of 1846, it marked an informal boundary between Mexico and the United States.

The price that travelers paid for the Cimarron Cut-off's brevity was steep. Referred to grimly as La Jornada del Muerto (The Journey of the Dead), the 60-mile cut-off was incredibly harsh. Screeching thunderstorms, sudden blizzards, drought, and interminable parched plains brought madness and even death to many traders and mountain men. (This route, though named the same, should not be confused with the desert area immediately east of the Rio Grande in southern New Mexico. That *jornada* was used by early Spanish traders from Mexico as a northbound shortcut to Santa Fe.)

If the fiery sun, terrible winds, or sandstorms didn't defeat travelers on the Jornada, there was still the serious threat of attack by Comanche and Kiowa war parties. Despite the fact that travelers must have cursed it, the Jornada del Muerto was the preferred route except during three periods—the Mexican War, the Civil War, and the trail's final days, when the Cimarron Cut-off was bypassed by the railroad.

Being roughly midway between Santa Fe and Independence, Cimarron signified the "point of no return." The crossing of the Arkansas River near Cimarron was known as the "middle crossing." It might cheer you up to reflect on the fact that, unlike the early Santa Fe travelers, you do not have to cross the Arkansas River. Large wagon trains took an entire day for this task. Though the Arkansas was shallow, it was a veritable minefield of dangers—a wide, raging current and a bottom full of quicksand and sinkholes. Once the wagons tipped in the holes, the animals panicked and became enmeshed in their lines. Everyone aboard would have to bail out, herd mules and oxen across the river, hitch fresh teams, and bodily drag the wagons free. A common sight, apparently, was the entire contents of a wagon spread out on the riverbanks to dry; in order to get the wagon out of the river, everything would have to be removed!

The two passages other than the Cimarron were the "lower crossing" in the vicinity of the present-day town of Ford and the "upper crossing" at Chouteau's Island. The "middle" or Cimarron crossing, which shifted locations slightly throughout the years, was the favorite of most traders.

Roughly 20 miles beyond Cimarron, you will pedal into Dodge City, also known as the "Cowboy Capital." After checking into your motel or establishing camp, plot out your tour of this touristy but nonetheless historic Old West town. Because this is a designated layover day in the twenty-one-day plan, there should be time to see both the authentic and Disneyesque parts of Dodge City.

The city's beginnings date back to 1865, one year after Fort Dodge was established. Soon the prairie town became a trade center for buffalo hunters and travelers. In the fall of 1872, the Atchison, Topeka and Santa Fe Railway reached the city.

Buffalo, which were a major source of revenue for Dodge City, were gone by 1876, but longhorn cattle from Texas filled in the gap. For the next decade, over five million head were driven up the Chisholm and Western trails to Dodge City. Cowboys acquired an unsavory reputation, and they avoided peace officers such as Bat Masterson and Wyatt Earp. Before Masterson and Earp and others of their ilk took over, lawlessness reigned and shootings abounded. The many shootings, in fact, necessitated the need for a local burial place, Boot Hill Cemetery.

Before seeing much of the city, however, it is a good idea to travel out by bike or rented car to **Fort Dodge**. The fort, located 5 miles east of Dodge City, has been maintained as a soldiers' home since 1889. The grassy lawns are graced with huge deciduous trees, and two of the original adobe barracks remain. Because they have been faced over with native stone, they do not look much like what they were during trail days.

Closer to its original state is Fort Dodge's post headquarters, named after that contentious military man, George Armstrong Custer. A pleasant two-story structure with a columned front porch and pitched red roof, the Custer House is now a private residence. After strolling or pedaling around the fort, return to Dodge City for a walking tour of historic landmarks.

Some highlights you will want to see include the following:

Located on the original site of Boot Hill Cemetery, the **Boot Hill Museum** brings the legend of the Old West to life. Dodge City's development is shown through audiovisual programs, exhibits, reconstructions, restorations, living history demonstrations, and theatrical performances. In summer, there are special offerings such as the melodrama and medicine show, the Long Branch Variety Show, stagecoach rides, gunfights, and a western chuck-wagon dinner.

Constructed in 1878 by Alonzo Webster, the **Hardesty House** is a graceful Victorian residence that was purchased by cattleman R. J. Hardesty in 1880. It is located at Boot Hill Museum.

At the turn of the century, a $7,500 grant from the Andrew Carnegie Foundation made the **Carnegie Library** possible. Listed on the National Register of Historic Sites, the building is now a community art center.

Built in 1900, the **Sughrue Home** was the home of a family by that name from 1915 to 1978. P. H. Sughrue, cousin of notable lawmen Pat and Mike Sughrue, was the city's deputy marshall in the early days. Though the house is not open for viewing, be sure to see it from the outside, noting especially the decorative ironwork in the patio and garden areas.

Begun in 1879 by bootmaker John Mueller, the native limestone **Home of Stone** is listed on the National Register of Historic Sites. It is operated by the Ford County Historical Society and open only during summer months.

Constructed in 1897, the **Santa Fe Depot** replaced an earlier depot that dates back to 1873. The present building also housed the Harvey House hotel and restaurant. It is not open for viewing.

Approximately 16 miles of Dodge City streets are brick. Note especially the cross-diagonal weave at intersections. This type of design was intended to prevent heavy vehicles from tearing up the street when making turns.

Dodge City boasts two annual events worthy of note: *Christmas in Dodge City* lights up "Old Front Street" with kerosene lamps, and features a community Christmas Tree lighting. *Summerfest*, July 4th, features fireworks and a gigantic entertainment extravaganza.

Kansas and More Kansas

Wagon rut marker, Cimarron Cut-off, Kansas.

Wagon ruts, eight miles west of Dodge City, Kansas.

Chapter Eleven

Kansas
Dodge City to Larned

Museum at Fort Larned National Historic Site, Kansas.

DAY 11 / 69 miles, 110 km

HIGHLIGHTS:
- ~ Sod House Museum
- ~ Fort Larned National Historic Site
- ~ Santa Fe Trail Center

Today's trek includes verdant farmland, Fort Larned, and the highly educational Santa Fe Trail Center. The road is flat and fast, and unless you encounter rainstorms, today's ride should be fairly easy. It is important to make good time, as you will want to allow as many hours as possible for touring Fort Larned and browsing through the Santa Fe Trail Center.

Leaving Dodge City by Highway 50, travel northeast through Spearville and Offerle to Kinsley, a distance of 20 miles. On both sides of the road, witness a colorful patchwork quilt of crops stretching as far as the eye can see: milo, corn, sorghum; fields of gold, tan, green, sage, and a multitude of hues in between. Because the area is so wide open, it can be as windblown as it is lovely. And as you must have discovered by now, the wind can produce an aching weariness unless you take breaks. The wind can also prove dangerous when gusty, especially if you are tired and your attention is less than normal. The truck stop at Spearville might be a good place for a snack and something hot to drink.

At Offerle, ~~you should pick up Highway 56, which~~ *continue on Highway 50 + 56 for 8 miles* ~~will take you in 8 miles to Kinsley, the next town~~ *to Kingsley, the next town on your route* on your route. If time allows, stop at the western limits of Kinsley at the town's roadside park. Of interest: a DAR marker next to a black railroad engine, and the **Sod House Museum**, a reminder of the first shelters built by immigrants after their arrival in this almost treeless prairie. After Kinsley, continue on Highway 56 to Garfield.

Very shortly after you pass through Garfield, there is a well-marked turnoff leading north to **Fort**

Larned National Historic Site. Once you have locked up your bike, prepare for a fascinating mental journey back to the Old West!

Fort Larned, like many of the Santa Fe Trail outposts, was moved several times before it settled in its final location. Originally called Camp on Pawnee Fort and Fort Alert, the settlement was established in 1859, the same year that the California gold rush ended. Its purpose was the protection of caravans, stagecoaches and travelers on the eastern leg of the Santa Fe Trail. In 1860, the fort was moved about 3 miles west and built out of a more lasting adobe. By 1868, the adobe was replaced with stone and timber.

Arranged in a quadrangle, the original nine buildings remain at Fort Larned today. To capture the flavor of life at this outpost, walk all around the quadrangle, going inside all the buildings that are open. Orient yourself at the barracks/visitor center by watching the audiovisual review of the trail's history. The film points out that, unlike Bent's Old Fort, Larned was important not so much for trade but as an escort station. After 1846 and the end of the war with Mexico, larger wagons could travel on the trail. Settlements such as Fort Larned played an essential role in protecting trading activities.

Take time to walk through the center's exhibits. Among the interesting facts you will acquire are that during trail days 75 million bison roamed North American plains! (Now in the United States and Canada there are only 155 thousand. Efforts are being made by animal conservationists to increase their number.) You learn that though the Santa Fe Trail is better known for beaver hides (which were used for the hats of that day), there was actually far more trade in buffalo skins.

After leaving the barracks/visitor center, walk clockwise to the post hospital, which, before becoming a hospital, housed one company of infantry and one of cavalry. The east half was converted to the post hospital in 1871. Next on your tour are the shops building (which housed a bakery and blacksmith shop) and a "new" and "old" commissary. In 1871, part of the new commissary was converted into a schoolroom for children living at the post.

After the commissaries, you will come to the quartermaster storehouse, with a large, open interior that was used as a warehouse. Stored in its cavernous depths were items needed for military operations: uniforms, bedding, tents, field gear, and tools.

Soldiers at Fort Larned lived an isolated and sometimes uncomfortable life. They were housed in tents at first, and the improvements—sod huts, dugouts, and adobe buildings—were only a slight improvement. After stone buildings were constructed in the 1860s, conditions became more tolerable.

The military diet was boring and unhealthy. Food that had been transported by wagon was often rancid, wormy, and spoiled. There were few fresh vegetables, and the men ate mainly hash, stew, bread, salt pork, and beans. Scurvy was rampant. Nearby "hog ranches," which supplied prostitutes and whiskey, flourished. During later years of the fort's occupation, the soldiers' escort duties of scouting expeditions, patrols along transportation lines, and campaigns against Indians were mostly over, and the post began to offer more amenities. It became more of a small village than a fort.

Much as Fort Lyon, near Bent's New Fort, guarded the eastern Colorado portion of the Santa Fe Trail, Fort Larned protected the Kansas segment. Its importance as a major guardian of Santa Fe Trail commerce can hardly be overestimated. Fort Larned soldiers cooperated with troops from Forts Union and Lyon. In the Indian War of 1868 to 1869, Fort Larned was a key post. Throughout the 1860s, it served as headquarters for the federal Indian Bureau.

Ironically, the final chapter in Fort Larned's history was its assistance in a development that brought about the demise of the very trail that it had guarded for so many years: the Santa Fe Railway. When the tracks made their way from Topeka in the early 1870s, soldiers at Fort Larned provided the construction workers with housing. By July 1878, the fort was nearly abandoned. After eighty years of private ownership, it was declared a national historic site in 1964.

Very near Fort Larned are excellent Santa Fe Trail ruts. In fact, the trail at this point, along with the fort itself, has been preserved as part of the historic site. The deeply worn furrows are surrounded by prairie grasses and a colony of prairie dogs. Ask at the visitor center for directions to the viewing area.

Already steeped in Santa Fe Trail lore, you will feel well prepared for the next attraction, the **Santa Fe Trail Center**. From the fort, head back to Highway 156, and pedal about 5 miles east to the Santa Fe Trail Center, a splendid regional museum that illustrates trail history from the time of prehistoric Indians to just after World War I. The center's exhibits include a fascinating series of period rooms depicting life in rural homes on the Plains. All three frontier cultures—Indian, Hispanic, and American—and their roles in shaping the Santa Fe Trail are well represented.

A small research library is available there, as well as archives of trail history and data. Throughout the years, special Santa Fe Trail events are held. The center is operated by Fort Larned, which also issues the newsletter *Trail Ruts*. For more information about special events, you can write ahead to: Director, Santa Fe Trail Center, Route 3, Larned, KS 67550.

When you leave the Santa Fe Trail Center, you will be on the outskirts of Larned. Pedal into town to your hotel or campsite.

Chapter Twelve

Kansas
Larned to Sterling

Quivira National Waterfowl Refuge, Seward, Kansas.

DAY 12 / 56 miles, 90 km

HIGHLIGHTS:
- Quivira National Waterfowl Refuge
- Pawnee Rock (side trip)

Leaving Larned via Broadway (which becomes Highway 19), you will cross both the Pawnee and Arkansas rivers. Staying on Highway 19 for 52 miles, proceed directly east.

Just after the turnoff to Seward, you will be passing through a particularly lovely stretch of countryside, the **Quivira National Waterfowl Refuge**. One of the U.S. Fish and Wildlife Service's systems of refuges, the area includes 21,820 acres of land rich in food and water sources for migratory fowl. In addition to two salt marshes, the refuge includes dozens of creeks, streams, and canals. It is a popular spot for camping, boating, fishing, and hunting.

There were, of course, earlier hunters in central Kansas—Indians. Then came the Spaniards, seeking not game but gold. The Spanish gold-seeking expeditions lasted from 1539 to 1542. Half a century after Columbus's discoveries in the "New World," Francisco Vásquez de Coronado and other Spanish explorers followed the Santa Fe Trail at least part of the way from northwest Mexico. Coronado and his *caballeros* (horsemen) were sent by Spain's viceroy to New Spain, now the southwestern United States. The purpose was the single-minded quest for gold, first at the mythical Seven Cities of Cíbola and then at the settlement of the Quiviran Indians.

Coronado was well-connected—governor of Nueva Galicia province and married to a relative of the king of Spain. The lust for gold was strong, and he was equipped mightily—his force included three hundred Spaniards, one thousand Indians, and twenty-five hundred horses. The cost was astronomical for those days: $125,000.

The cities of gold receded into the distance, for when Coronado's expedition reached Cíbola—now identified as the pueblos of northeastern New Mexico—there was no gold. The Indians told Coronado and his men that the riches they were seeking could be found to the north in the "Kingdom of Quivira." Coronado pushed onward with a smaller army, and several Indians included as guides. Soon, however, they became lost, and historians note that there is a strong possibility that the guides had led Coronado astray purposely simply to get him out of the pueblos.

In his quest to reach Quivira, Coronado eventually reached the area around the present-day Lyons and found the Quiviran Indians. Still, no gold. It seems as though Coronado chose not to believe tales of gold further north, in Pawnee Indian country, but chose instead to spend nearly a month in Quivira. He visited several dozen villages before returning to Mexico and Spain. The Franciscan friar traveling with him—Father Juan Padilla—felt called to stay among the Quivirans to teach them Christianity, an act of devotion that cost him his life. He was the first Christian martyr in North America.

When you reach Highways 14 north and 96 west, approximately 30 miles after the turnoff to Seward, turn left (directly north) on Highways 14 and 96. Pedal into Sterling and settle into your campsite or hotel for the evening.

....

SIDE TRIP SUGGESTION delete whole section

Since you haven't had to stop for many roadside attractions on this fairly level 56-mile ride, there may be enough time to finish out the afternoon with a 36-mile roundtrip to **Pawnee Rock**.

Ten miles north of Sterling is Lyons, and if you go northeast of Lyons for 8 miles on Highway 56, you can view famous Pawnee Rock, the major natural landmark on the Kansas segment of the Santa Fe Trail. It was both a campground for wagon trains and, ironically, an Indian ambush site. Nearly everyone who traveled and wrote about the Santa Fe Trail included a description of this small hill with a rock face.

Susan Magoffin's diary entry of July 4, 1846, reads as follows:

> We went up and while *mi alma* [her husband] with his gun and pistols kept watch, for the wily Indian may always be apprehended here, it is a good lurking place and they are ever ready to fall upon any unfortunate trader behind his company . . . I cut my name, among the many hundreds inscribed on the rock and many of whom I knew.

Sorghum and silos, Lyons, Kansas.

Chapter Thirteen

Kansas
Sterling to Hillsboro

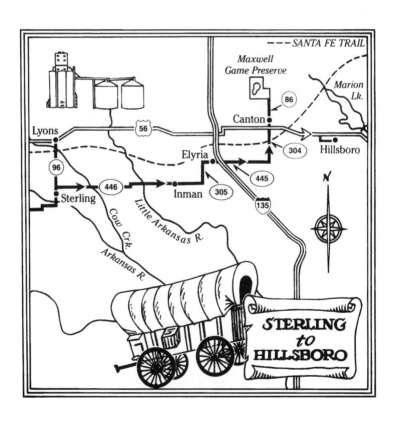

Adobe House Museum, Hillsboro, Kansas.

DAY 13 / 67 miles, 107 km

HIGHLIGHTS:
- Olde Town
- Adobe House Museum

An appropriate pastime during today's longish trek might be to estimate the distance from one grain elevator to the next. For many miles, they will be your only landmarks.

Pedal east out of Sterling on East Cleveland Road for 15½ miles—at the time of this writing the road was also marked Detour 96 for the first 6⅓ miles, and you should continue *east* when Detour 96 turns off—to the end of the pavement. At this point you should turn north (left) on Highway 304 for 8 miles to Highway 56 at Windom. When you come to Highway 56, turn east (right) for the rest of today's journey.

With many miles to cover, a peaceful road to follow, and few landmarks to note, this stretch provides a delightful opportunity to reflect on the life and times of the trail travelers over a century ago. Although William Becknell is canonized as the father of the Santa Fe Trail, many had crossed Kansas before him. After all, to Coronado and his adventurers, Kansas was the fabled Quivira. And after Coronado's unsuccessful treasure hunt in 1541, Frenchmen from the Illinois country were driven west by an insatiable lust for trade and adventure. Some writers seem to feel that Zebulon M. Pike should receive the greatest recognition for opening the Santa Fe Trail. The journal of his travels between Santa Fe and Chihuahua, Mexico—which took place from 1806 to 1807—made American traders aware of the great potential profit in interaction with northern Mexico.

Until this time Spain had denied its subjects in New Spain any trade with the U.S., but when Mexico gained independence from Spain in 1821, permission for U.S. trade with Mexico's province of Nuevo Mexico was not slow in coming. And the Mexicans in Nuevo Mexico were quick to recognize that trade with the U.S. would not only provide many things not available from Mexico, but would also drive down the inflated prices for goods brought from Ciudad Chihuahua to Santa Fe.

The Santa Fe Trail was created for and sustained by trade. January 29, 1822, is generally accepted as the opening of the trail. It was on that day that four men arrived in Franklin, Missouri, having traveled all the way from San Miguel (50 miles south of Santa Fe) with bags of silver pesos. News of their wealth spread like wildfire, and the enterprising, ambitious, and adventurous were lured westward on the Santa Fe Trail.

By the 1830s, the routine for Santa Fe Trail caravans was well established, and it changed little from year to year. Preparations for an expedition began during the winter, when traders bought goods in Philadelphia or St. Louis. All spring, steamboats brought goods up the Missouri River to Independence Landing. In early May, Independence was teeming with merchants, suppliers, traders, and drivers. Outlying towns were filled with wagons and animals being trained for the upcoming trip. As they whipped the mules into obedience, muleteers also provided a spectacle for crowds of onlookers.

The height of prairie grasses provided the starting date for the wagon trains. When the grasses grew tall enough to provide forage for the mules and oxen, the wagons were packed with goods for sale as well as supplies for the journey—flour, bacon, sugar, coffee, salt, and beans. Once the trains left for the prairies, meat and fuel (dried droppings) would be provided by the buffalo.

A journalist of the time, Matt Field, described the scene in 1839:

Suppose the starting of a caravan for Santa Fe. In the square you observe a number of enormous wagons into which men are packing bales and boxes. Presently the mules are driven in from pasture, and a busy time commences in the square, catching the fractious animals with halters and introducing them to harness for their long journey. Full half a day is thus employed before the expedition finally gets into motion and winds slowly out of town. This is an exciting moment. Every window sash is raised, and anxious faces appear watching with interest the departure. The drivers snap their long whips and swear at their unruly mules, bidding goodbye in parentheses between the oaths, to old friends on each side of the street as they move along.

[*Chronicles of Oklahoma 37* (1960): 310–22.]

Ten miles east of Canton, look for the road that turns right just before the railroad crossing. This is "Old Highway 56." It parallels new Highway 56, but is less traveled. Take it for the remaining 2 miles into Hillsboro.

Marc Simmons, in *Following the Santa Fe Trail,* describes this town as "one of the tidiest and most energetic towns in Kansas." It hosts festivals in spring and fall, and there is a handsome building, circa 1887, called **Olde Town**, which contains an interesting collection of shops. On the left (south) side of Highway 56 as you enter Hillsboro, be sure to stop at the **Adobe House Museum**, which gives a fascinating glimpse of Mennonite culture in the town's early days. The rooms are well decorated with folk art, furnishings, kitchen items, and clothing of the time. If you have time, stop by the chamber of commerce at 102 Main (or write or call in advance; see appendix) for maps and brochures of the area to seek out more historic points of interest.

The sag wagon.

Chapter Fourteen

Kansas
Hillsboro to Council Grove

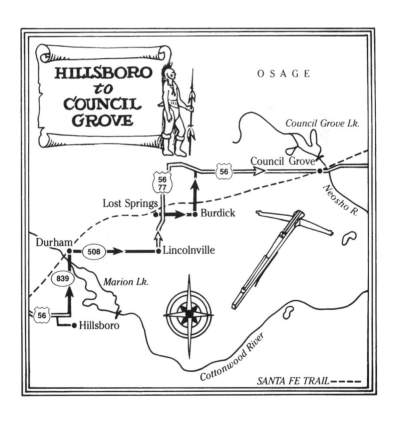

Last Chance Store, Council Grove, Kansas.

DAYS 14 and 15 / 63 miles, 101 km
(LAYOVER DAY)

HIGHLIGHTS:
- Council Oak Shrine
- Post Office Oak
- Madonna of the Trail
- Hays House
- Last Chance Store
- Neosho Bridge
- Old Kaw Mission/Museum

Leave Hillsboro on Old Highway 56, and when you are nearly 2 miles east of Hillsboro, turn left (north) on Highway 839. This is a Kansas country road at its best—scant traffic; birds singing; sorghum, milo, corn, and alfalfa fields in every direction. After about 10 miles, you will pass through Marion Lake country, with green rolling hills—a refreshing change after the long flat plains in most of Kansas.

When you reach Highway 508, turn right and bicycle directly east to Lincolnville. If you happen to be cycling through this charming small town in early October, you might be lucky enough to chance upon the annual Octoberfest. The community celebration, held right on Main Street, is a wonderful combination of bake sale, crafts emporium, flea market, and talent show.

Take Highway 77 due north out of Lincolnville and travel northward to Lost Springs (which is off to the left of Highway 77). This is a good spot for lunch if you packed food for today; if you did not bring food along, there may or may not be food available in Lost Springs.

Take the only road leading east out of Lost Springs to Burdick. Just before Burdick take Main Street north, back to Highway 56. When you reach 56, take a sharp turn east and bicycle into Council Grove. Located on the Neosho River, Council Grove is not only one of the most historic towns you will encounter on the Santa Fe Trail, it is also one whose monuments are best documented and preserved.

This is an official layover, with a lot to see, so after you are settled into your camp or hotel, you might want to begin exploring on your first day here. Council Grove has an excellent marked historic walking tour. Its chamber of commerce brochures bill Council Grove as the "birthplace of the Santa Fe Trail." The river, abundant timber, and ample pasture are great attractions.

By thoughtfully considering the name Council Grove, you will gain considerable insight into the town. The "grove" refers, of course, to the trees that grew in abundance along the Neosho River—hickory, oak, and walnut. Their welcome shade and coolness provided a watershed separating the rolling prairies from the vast Great Plains area that lie beyond on the route to Santa Fe. After Council Grove, there would be no more hardwood trees growing. Traders would load up on spare axles and stow them under their wagons. After the town was established in the 1850s, Council Grove continued to be a place to stock up. Travelers bought arms, supplies and tools before setting off across the plains.

The "council" in the town's name refers to the 1825 treaty made between government survey commissioners and the Osage Indians. The agreement ensured safe passage of caravans through Indian territory. Included among the famous who camped in the Council Grove area were Kit Carson and General George Armstrong Custer.

The jagged stump of the historic oak tree under which the treaty was sealed is preserved in a type of shrine and surrounded by a park. In addition to the historic agreement with the Osage people, the town offered a meeting and rendezvous place for Santa Fe Trail traders, mountain men, and anyone who might be happening to travel the trail.

Thanks in large part to civic pride and the diligent efforts of history-minded trail aficionados, the Council Grove walking tour is delightful. Check with the chamber of commerce for a numbered brochure. Even after two weeks of cycling, the walk is not taxing. In fact, it will give you a good chance to stretch out your tightened muscles. Everything is within easy strolling distance. Not to be missed are the following:

Only the trunk remains at the **Council Oak Shrine**, site of the signing of the safe-passage treaty with the Osage Indians. A DAR marker and interpretive historical sign add interest to the spot.

A cache at the bottom of a hug oak tree called **Post Office Oak** is said to have served as a post office for pack trains and caravans from 1825 to 1847. Letters left by trail travelers at the bottom of the tree were picked up and carried by returning caravans back to the states.

Kansas is one of the twelve states in which the DAR has erected commemorative monuments to the intrepid women who ventured forth on America's early trails and forged homesteads in the west. The Council Grove **Madonna of the Trail** is situated on the site of an old Santa Fe Trail campground. The massive cement and stone pioneer mother, babe in arm, is flanked by a small boy and is holding a rifle. She is one of several Madonnas of the Trail enshrined along the route. Note her sunbonnet, a women's fashion that continued till the middle of this century; her face, peering out from the bonnet, seems to wear an expression of strength and serenity.

The inscription at the base of this striking monument reads:

> Into the primitive west,
> Face upflung toward the sun,
> Bravely she came,

Her children beside her
Here she made them a home,
Beautiful pioneer mother!

To the pioneer mother of America,
Through whose courage and sacrifice
The desert has blossomed,
The camp became the home
The blazed trail the thorofare (sic).

Built in 1857 by Seth Hays, a great-grandson of Daniel Boone and cousin of Kit Carson, the **Hays House** is a historic building, which has been altered radically from the original. Little remains that is authentic. The site has served as a theater, a court of law, a church social hall, a caravan outfitter's store, and a tavern. Today it houses an excellent restaurant.

The **Last Chance Store** was a local trading place for Indians to exchange pelts for supplies and also a last chance for travelers west to Santa Fe to load up on beans, bacon, and whiskey. It has been used as a curio shop but is now closed.

The **Neosho Bridge**, at the intersection of Highway 56 and Main Street, is placed at the original trail crossing. The stands of hardwood trees from which the pioneers made spare wagon parts still remain to the north and south of Council Grove.

The **Old Kaw Mission/Museum**, built around 1850 by the Methodist Episcopal Mission, is a handsome stone building that served first as an Indian school, then as a school for the white children of Council Grove. Today it is a state museum housing thousands of artifacts from pioneer life.

Chapter Fifteen

Kansas
Council Grove to Baldwin City

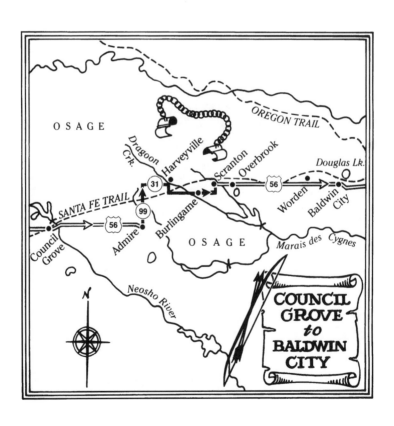

Dragoon Creek crossing, Harveyville, Kansas.

DAY 16 / 80 miles, 128 km

HIGHLIGHTS:
- Dragoon Creek crossing
- Burlingame ("Council City")
- The Old Castle

Today's trek, though not difficult, is quite long. The Flint Hills, encountered as you bicycle eastward from Council Grove, add variety to the terrain but also call quite heavily on the quadriceps. An early start and regular stretching along the route are advisable today. You should pack especially well, making sure you are prepared for blistering heat or icy rain. In the same day, it is entirely possible you will encounter both.

Leave Council Grove via Main Street (which is also Highway 56). Then pedal straight east for 22 miles. Those who claim that all of Kansas is checkerboard flat have never traveled through the Flint Hills of eastern Kansas. Lovely green undulating hills, they go on for miles. Rather than taxing, you may well find them refreshing. Experts advise that when pedaling uphill you will get more power if you pull upward with the top of one foot against the toe-clips while pushing downward with the other.

When you come to Highway 99, go north about 9 miles, where you will reach Highway 31. Go through Harveyville, where Highway 31 takes a jog right for 2 miles and then turns left (east) once again. Along with Burlingame, which you will reach soon, Harveyville played a key role in the anti-slavery movement. Henry Harvey's loft was a station for slaves traveling by the "underground railroad" to freedom in the North.

After Harveyville, continuing east, you will come to a DAR marker commemorating the **Dragoon Creek crossing**. Across the road from the marker is a field, all that is left of the Havana stage station.

Founded in 1858 by German and French settlers and now just a field, Havana in its heyday boasted a store and hotel.

In another 1½ miles, you will come to the crossing itself. Apparently the creek gained its name in 1852 when a mounted infantry company crossed over it.

Pedaling on, you will soon reach **Burlingame**, entered via a lovely downhill stretch of road that becomes the town's main street. The town boasts several good cafes and restaurants—an ideal place to stop and have lunch.

As you enjoy a well-earned break from the road, you might want to reflect on the history of Burlingame. The high point of Santa Fe Trail traffic probably was reached during the Pike's Peak gold rush of 1859, when as many as five hundred wagons passed through Burlingame in a single day (compared to a pre-gold rush day with twenty-five wagons daily).

Founded in 1857, the town was originally named Council City. Much in the fashion of Council Grove, it was apparently a gathering place for traders and travelers, who refreshed themselves as their mules were being shod before the long trip west to Santa Fe, or their return to Independence, Missouri.

Tradition has it that the Santa Fe Trail went down Burlingame's Main Street, though some historians claim that wagon trains actually went around Main Street. There is also a popular local claim that Burlingame is where "rails and trail meet," but disclaimers point out that by the time the railroad came to Burlingame, the wagon trains bound for Santa Fe were long gone. The town's namesake is Anson Burlingame, famous as an anti-slavery advocate and as an ambassador to China.

Leaving Burlingame, continue east on Highway 31, which joins Highway 56. Take Highway 56, turning 2 miles north (left) into Scranton, then right (east) all the way to Baldwin City. As with several other Santa Fe Trail settlements, Baldwin City was first named something else. Founded in 1854, "Palmyra" was a wagon stop that grew prosperous from trail traffic. Travelers could be sure of finding supplies, blacksmith and wagon repair shops, and plenty of company.

Another interesting fact about Palmyra/Baldwin City is its location. The town was built immediately west of The Narrows, a strip of high ground running between Marais des Cygnes River to the south and Wakarusa Creek to the north. During periods of heavy rain, wagons would become hopelessly mired in deep mud unless they stayed on the hump of dry ground between the two boggy areas—hence the name "Narrows." Nothing remains of The Narrows today except an uninteresting hump of ground.

Baldwin City claims the Kansas Territory's first college, Baker. As if realizing that their town must have more going for it than trail-traffic trade, they founded Baker College in 1858. The institution's first building, **The Old Castle**, which houses a museum, is located on 5th Street between Elm and Fremont, south of Highway 56. The museum contains items from the nearby villages—now ghost towns—of Palmyra, Black Jack, Prairie City, and Media. Exhibits include copies of *McGuffey's Reader*, hand-drawn maps of the Santa Fe Trail and surroundings, glassed-in copies of America's first newspaper, and collections of Indian tools and arrowheads. It is open afternoons from Tuesday through Saturday.

Actual Santa Fe Trail conestoga wagon, Kearny County
Historical Museum, Kansas (see p.73).

We're Not in Kansas Anymore

River overlook from Lexington battlefield, Missouri.

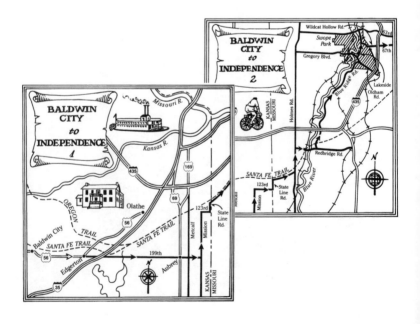

Chapter Sixteen

Kansas & Missouri
Baldwin City to Independence

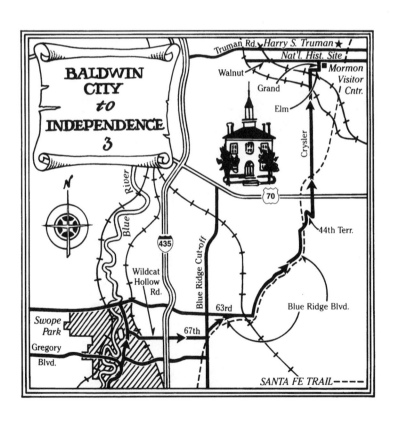

Madonna of the Trail, Lexington, Missouri.

Independence Courthouse, Missouri.

DAY 17 / 70 miles, 112 km

HIGHLIGHTS:
- Independence Courthouse Square
- Truman Courthouse
- Bingham–Waggoner House
- National Frontier Trails Center
- Santa Fe Trail Park

Bicycling from Baldwin City to Independence involves navigating Kansas City, which is one of the most interesting but difficult stretches of bicycling along the Santa Fe Trail. In the words of Willard Chilcott, organizer of the first-known Santa Fe to New Franklin bicycle trek, "It's murderous but do-able."

The highlights are listed for those who choose to spend an extra day in Independence. If you are following a strict twenty-one-day schedule, you may have time for only one or two at best.

Leave Baldwin City by Highway 56. Turn east (right) for a 17-mile stretch to Edgerton. Just after Edgerton, where Highway 56 curves north, make a more-than-90-degree turn off to the right onto 199th Street.

Go for 20 miles on 199th Street. Pass Metcalf and take a left (north) turn onto the next street after Metcalf, which is Mission. Continue north on Mission for 9½ miles.

Take a right on 123rd Street and pedal until it ends at Stateline Road. Turn left (north) on Stateline and go a short distance to Santa Fe Trail. Turn right (east) onto Santa Fe Trail, part of the original route. Continue until the road ends at Holmes Road.

Take a left at Holmes and head north until you reach Red Bridge Road, where you will take a right turn and head east.

Continue east on Red Bridge until you reach Blue River Road. Continue north on Blue River into Swope Park.

Once you reach Swope Park, be sure to plan ahead using your map. There are no street signs in the park. Take a left on Oldham Road, a right on Gregory Boulevard, a left on Lakeside Drive, and a right on Wild Cat Hollow Drive, which becomes 67th Street. Make sure to take 67th rather than nearby 63rd Street.

Continue pedaling east on 67th Street to Blue Ridge Boulevard. Take a left on Blue Ridge Boulevard as it continues north. When you come to 47th Street, jog right (east) and then left (north) to 44th Street.

Turn right on 44th Street and then left (north) on Crysler. Continue north on Crysler to Elm; take a right on Elm, a left on Grand, and a right on Walnut. The Mormon Center is located at 932 West Walnut. This is a good place to get your bearings, even if you are not planning to camp at their site.

If your schedule allows, Independence, the "Queen City of the Trails," is worthy of an extra day of exploration and soaking up history. For the first three decades of the trail, it was the outfitting point for Santa Fe trade. From New York, Philadelphia, St. Louis, and Europe, merchandise arrived by steamboat to this bustling metropolis. Goods were then transferred from boats to Santa Fe-bound wagons. Along with actual traders, there were many other businessmen who thrived here: livestock and mule salesmen, wagon and harness makers, blacksmiths, local merchants, and livery stable owners.

Independence was frequented by frontiersman Kit Carson; Josiah Gregg, author of *Commerce of the Prairies*; and famous diarist Susan Magoffin. Gregg's book (1844) was the first to publicize the trail.

Gregg's first knowledge of the trail came secondhand—from his father, who accompanied William Becknell on an expedition. In later life, the young Josiah experienced the trail for nine years as a Santa Fe trader. Despite his bout with tuberculosis, Gregg joined a caravan to Santa Fe and operated very successfully as a frontier merchant. His book on the trail appeared just a few years after he left the trade. It is possible that Gregg, because he was a medical doctor, knew the beneficial effects of dry desert air on consumptive lungs; he insisted on joining his first expedition despite the fact that (according to a personal friend's observation) he was so sickly he could not mount his horse. Gregg's often-quoted book provides a vital part of Santa Fe Trail history.

If you have time after checking into your lodging for the night, here are some highlights that will enhance your visit to Independence:

Independence Courthouse Square, located at the corner of Liberty and Lexington, was the springboard from which trail expeditions began. Only the ghosts of the original buildings remain. At the corner of Liberty and Maple, now occupied by a parking lot, sat the popular Nebraska House, built in 1849. Another popular hostelry in the vicinity was the Merchants Hotel. The building presently on the site (at the northwest corner of Main and Maple) is said to incorporate some parts of the original building. Independence Square is where the trail split into two branches; one went to Westport and another headed south to Raytown. The branches joined together at New Santa Fe on the Kansas–Missouri border.

Situated at 112 West Lexington, the **Truman Courthouse** includes some parts of earlier Jackson County courthouses that date back to trail days. It is now called the Truman Courthouse, recalling Truman's office there in the 1920s and 1930s. A large equestrian statue of Andrew Jackson, the county's namesake, looms to the west of the courthouse. Near the site are two DAR markers, one for the Santa Fe Trail and another for the Oregon Trail's beginning. The Oregon Trail procession began in the early 1840s as part of a migration of pioneers from the Middle West to the Pacific Northwest. Missionaries played a role in the first permanent settlements in the Northwest. The Oregon Territory was annexed by the United States in 1846.

Located at 313 West Pacific, the historic **Bingham–Waggoner House** is owned by Independence and is open to the public. Jacob Hall, a prominent freighter in Chihuahua and Santa Fe trade, was one of the earliest owners of the property. John Lewis, a saddlemaker associated with the Santa Fe trade, was a later owner. Finally, after several other owners, the estate was purchased by highly respected George Caleb Bingham, a Missouri artist who resided there with his wife for six years. The final private owners were Peter and William Waggoner and their descendants, after which the property went to the city of Independence.

Across the street from the Bingham–Waggoner House is the new **National Frontier Trails Center**, which should probably not be missed.

At **Santa Fe Trail Park,** just off Santa Fe Road and a block north of 31st Street, traces can still be found of trail ruts that were cut by the passage of caravans departing from Courthouse Square. An especially interesting trail remnant is located to the north of the park's baseball diamond. In the creek that runs next to the diamond is a dirt ramp with a low stone retaining wall. This is believed to date back to the Santa Fe Trail era.

Chapter Seventeen

Missouri
Independence to Lexington

INDEPENDENCE
to
LEXINGTON

- - - - SANTA FE TRAIL

Fort Osage, Sibley, Missouri.

DAY 18 / 45 miles, 72 km

HIGHLIGHTS:
- Fort Osage
- Sibley Cemetery
- Battle of Lexington State Park
- Lexington Historical Museum
- Lafayette County Courthouse
- Madonna of the Trail Monument
- 1830s Log Cabin

Leaving Independence can be a bit nerve-wracking, but before long, you will be traveling lovely country roads. Depart from your camp or hotel and proceed to Truman Road. If you are leaving the Mormon visitor center, your route out of town will be Pleasant Road north to Truman Road. Turn right (east) on Truman to Powell.

Take a left (north) on Powell and stay on it approximately 5 miles. Travel north on Powell until you come to Highway 24, where you will turn left for a short distance, then right onto Blue Mills Road.

Continuing on Blue Mills Road, in about 5 miles you will come to a sign on the left to Sibley and Fort Osage. Follow the signs to Osage, and try to allow a couple hours for exploring this important historic landmark. From U.S. Highway 24, you will proceed north on Country Road 20 a few miles to the fort. Just follow the signs.

Fort Osage, now restored to its original appearance, was, for a few years in the 1820s, the westernmost Santa Fe Trail outpost. Established in 1808 by explorer William Clark (of Lewis and Clark fame), it perches atop a high bluff overlooking the Missouri River. Like most of the forts on the Santa Fe Trail, Fort Osage served at various times as a military garrison and an Indian trading post. It was an official government fur-trading post.

George Sibley, whose name occurs frequently in trail lore, was a major Fort Osage personage. Both trader and United States commissioner, Sibley surveyed the Santa Fe Trail in 1825.

If you like browsing through old cemeteries, you might want to take a side trip to the **Sibley Cemetery**, located to the right of the Fort Osage visitor center. Note the grave of Zenas Leonard, a famous fur trapper and author of a narrative of Zenas Leonard. Also of interest is a ramp leading down from a DAR marker to the Missouri River. It was originally used by trail wagons making their cumbersome way up from the landing.

The visitor center is a must: it offers exhibits that show and tell history of local Indians and the fort itself. George Sibley and his wife resided there briefly, and their quarters are furnished in the style of the period. Shelves in the modern-day "trading post" are stocked with goods that replicate those of trail days, and costumed guides add to the feeling of going back in time.

Leaving Fort Osage, return to Blue Mills Road and work your way back to Highway 24. Go left for 1½ miles and right for 2 miles. You will travel east on Highway 24 for 6 miles before reaching Highway 224, at which point you will veer left. Proceed on Highway 224 through Napoleon, Wellington, and into Lexington.

After settling into your lodging or campsite for the night, take time to explore Lexington, a gracious town more reminiscent of the antebellum South than the western frontier. Perched on a bluff overlooking the Missouri River's south bank, it is graced with old homes, tree-lined streets, shops, and restaurants.

Settled in the early 1820s, Lexington soon became a prosperous farming community and river town. Many homes and buildings constructed during the 1840s and 1850s are still there.

The first steamboat, *Western Engineer*, ventured up the Missouri River to Lexington's landing. The Aull Brothers Mercantile Firm, a veritable Sears Roebuck of the time, was headquartered in Lexington, with branch stores in Independence, Liberty, and Richmond. Throughout the 1830s, Lexington outfitters supplied a steady stream of wagons with merchandise, mules, and oxen.

During the Civil War, pro-South forces captured the town in the 1861 Battle of Lexington. If you have time, visit the **Battlefield of Lexington State Park**, located off Utah Street. The battlefield contains remnants of Union breastworks and trenches. The 105-acre historic site includes the Anderson House, built in 1853 and used by both Union and Confederate forces as a field hospital during the battle; this was where surrender to the Confederates took place. The house has been restored in mid- to late-nineteenth century style, and is open daily to the public. A small admission fee includes a thirty-minute tour of the house.

Other points of interest in Lexington include the following:

The **Lexington Historical Museum**, built as a Presbyterian church in 1846, contains Pony Express memorabilia, Battle of Lexington items, and a good collection of old Lexington photographs. For Civil War buffs there is a fifteen-minute slide presentation on the Battle of Lexington. The museum is open afternoons from June to November.

Lafayette County Courthouse, situated on Main Street between Tenth and Eleventh, was a sight familiar to Santa Fe Trail travelers in the 1850s. Of special interest is the clock tower, formed of four columns. In the east column is lodged a cannonball fired during the Battle of Lexington. Also note the bronze Pony Express plaque with busts of Russell, Majors, and Waddell at the northwest corner of the grounds.

Lexington's **Madonna of the Trail Monument** is one of several identically cast pioneer madonna statues along the Santa Fe Trail and other immigrant routes. This shrine is located near Broadway on a bluff above the Missouri River. The statue is eighteen feet tall and inscribed on all four faces of the base. Next to the monument is a granite DAR marker.

An **1830s Log Cabin**, located between Broadway and Main, has been restored and furnished by the Lexington Historical Association in keeping with imagined family life during trail days. It is the only known non-brick structure still standing from Lexington's early days, and is open daily for touring. Specially arranged tours are available by writing to the Lexington Chamber of Commerce, Tourism Committee (see appendix).

Lexington Historical Museum, Missouri.

Chapter Eighteen

Missouri
Lexington to Arrow Rock

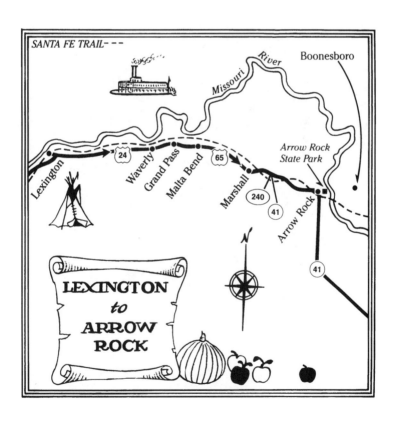

Main Street, Arrow Rock, Missouri.

DAY 19 / 57 miles, 91 km

HIGHLIGHTS:
- Old Tavern
- Santa Fe Spring
- Lyceum Theatre
- Arrow Rock Masonic Lodge
- Sappington Memorial Building and Museum
- Arrow Rock Historic Site Museum

There is so much to see in Arrow Rock that an early start is advised for today's easy ride. You will be going alongside and interconnecting with the Santa Fe Trail quite closely, and also passing through scenic, verdant countryside. If you are cycling the trail in summer or fall, be prepared for lots of fruit stands offering nuts, honey, sorghum, cider, pumpkins, squash, apples, and pickles. It is fun to stop occasionally to buy healthy snacks and talk with people running the stands. After all, meeting people along the road is a major advantage of traveling the Santa Fe Trail by bike, and—history aside—these encounters are likely to provide some of your best memories.

Departing from your Lexington camp area or lodgings, return to Highway 224 and go east. In about 2 miles, Highway 224 will merge with Highway 24.

Pedaling eastward, continue on Highway 24 approximately 17 miles to Waverly, where Highway 24 will join Highway 65. Continue on Highway 65 through the small towns of Grand Pass (population 71) and Malta Bend (population 200), and on to Marshall (population 12,781). Once inside Marshall city limits, turn left on Business Highway 65, which merges with Highway 240 and Highway 41, and go through the north part of Marshall. It is smooth sailing from here on: Highway 41 will bring you to Arrow Rock in a pleasant 15 miles.

After you have settled into hotel or camp and freshened up, prepare to walk or pedal around a town that has witnessed the passage of several eras of American history.

Originally named New Philadelphia (before it was part of the Santa Fe Trail), Arrow Rock was an Indian rendezvous spot. The town was mentioned in the Lewis and Clark journals of 1804 and in their 1819 Yellowstone Expedition account. By 1815, permanent settlers arrived, followed by immigrants from Kentucky and Virginia. When a Missouri River ferry was established, it strengthened the town's importance as a trading center for area farmers and as an outfitting town for Santa Fe Trail expeditions.

Virginian John Huston was an important person in the town's history. In 1834, he built the **Old Tavern**, which today as in the past serves fine home-cooked meals to travelers. The tavern is full of portraits and relics of early residents, and a historical brochure is available in the tavern's foyer.

The population decline in Arrow Rock tells a story similar to that of many towns along the trail. Its population hit a peak in the mid-1800s with over one thousand residents, but the number has since declined to eighty. After the demise of the Santa Fe Trail and the birth of the railroad, Arrow Rock's importance as a transportation link literally vanished. Westward-heading railroads bypassed the town, and major highway bridges were located many miles to the south.

Arrow Rock's history is rich. Among its noted citizens, it counts artist George Caleb Bingham; medical doctor John Sappington, famous for his work in treating malaria; and three Missouri governors—Meredith Marmeduke, Clairborne Jackson, and John Marmeduke.

A note about Dr. Sappington. Beginning in 1832, he became famous for his "Anti-Fever Pills," the only preventative at the time for malaria. The pills contained gum myrrh, licorice, and a grain of quinine. Carried by mosquitoes, malaria—or "ague"—was prevalent in western Missouri and eastern Kansas, especially along the Arkansas River and in Council Grove. Sappington's 1844 treatise, *The Theory and Treatment of Fevers*, revealed the formula for the pills. Sappington's pill-roller and medicine case are on display in the Old Tavern.

In addition to the tavern, sights not to be missed include the following:

Santa Fe Spring, also known as Arrow Rock Spring and Big Spring, is two blocks beyond the Old Tavern and in a picnic area. The spring is where Santa Fe-bound wagons assembled after leaving the nearby river landing.

The **Lyceum Theatre**, built in 1872 as a Baptist church, is a Gothic Revival building now serving as a summer theatre. The usual summer repertory includes six plays presented evenings from Wednesday through Sunday. For information, write or call the Arrow Rock Lyceum (see appendix).

The **Arrow Rock Masonic Lodge**, on Main Street, 1½ blocks west of the tavern, was founded in 1842. Records show that it sent some of its members over the Santa Fe Trail on expeditions. Today the first floor of the lodge is used as a center for arts and crafts.

The **Sappington Memorial Building and Museum**, at the end of High Street and next door to the Lyceum, is worthy of a stop if you have time.

Arrow Rock Historic Site Museum, recently completed, contains photographs and artifacts from Arrow Rock's early history.

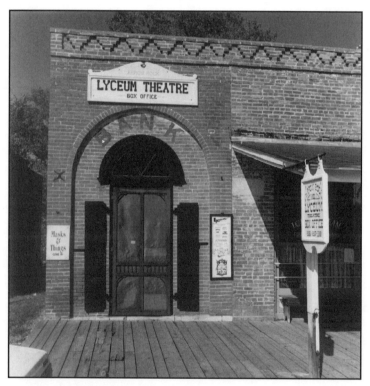

Lyceum Theatre, Arrow Rock, Missouri.

Chapter Nineteen

Missouri
Arrow Rock to New Franklin

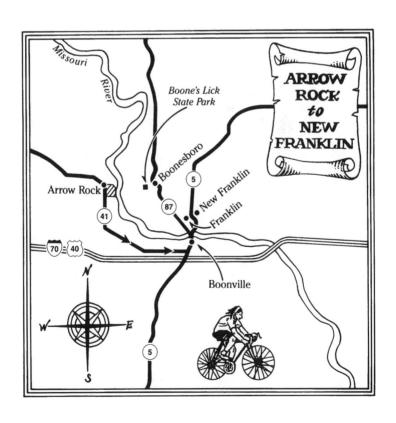

Old bridge near "Old" Franklin Monument, Missouri.

DAYS 20 and 21 / 45 miles, 72 km
(RECOVERY DAY)

HIGHLIGHTS:
- ⇀ Boonville
- ⇀ Boone's Lick
- ⇀ "The Beginning of the Trail" monument
- ⇀ Peter B. Harris–J. Warren Chilton Home
- ⇀ Old Seminary

Highway 41, which begins today's easy ride, takes you south out of Arrow Rock on rolling hills. Handcraft Farm (Rose Hill) is about 6 miles. Rose Hill Farm features handcrafted items. Continue on this lovely road as it curves eastward and approaches I-70. it becomes a frontage road paralleling the main highway.

Travel east about 5 miles on the frontage road until you come to the intersection with Highways 70, 40, and 5 at a car dealership, where you must take a left (north). This takes you into **Boonville**, 3 miles away, a town established in 1817 and named after Daniel Boone. Though of minor importance in Santa Fe Trail trade, Boonville is mentioned as a starting point for the trail trade in its early years. Like other trail towns along the Missouri, Boonville had a landing for steamboats bringing goods from St. Louis: a cobblestone street ascended the slope from the docks to the warehouses.

Even though there are some interesting old buildings in Boonville—Christ Episcopal Church, dating from 1846; Thespian Hall, begun in 1855; and Kemper Military School, founded in 1844—there are no buildings still standing that relate directly to the Santa Fe Trail.

At Boonville, you will cross the wide Missouri River on a steel bridge. A narrow ramp on the right is intended for pedestrians and cyclists. If car and foot traffic is heavy on the main part of the bridge, you may prefer to walk rather than ride across.

Immediately after crossing the river, you will come to Highway 87. Turning left (west), proceed on Highway 87 towards Boonesboro. Pass through Boonesboro and cycle about 1 mile north. On Route 87 you will see a sign on the left which leads to **Boone's Lick,** on Route 187, now a Missouri state park, 3½ miles from Boonesboro.

The famous spring that created Boone's Lick now contains very little salt, but when Daniel Boone's sons Nathan and Daniel established their salt business here in 1805, they were able to produce twenty-five to thirty bushels of salt daily. The process was simple: they brought water to a boil in large iron kettles; after the water evaporated, salt crystals remained. The business expanded from eight to twenty helpers and from one to four furnaces, and at its peak was able to produce one hundred bushels of salt daily. One bushel or fifty pounds of salt brought $2 to $2.50.

In its heyday, Boone's Lick attracted settlers from the East. It was closely tied in with the original city of Franklin, a town that could rightly be called the hub of the frontier.

After you have seen Boone's Lick, to get to New Franklin simply retrace your route back 10 miles along Highways 87 (south) to Highway 5. Take a left (north) at the juncture of Highways 87 and 5, and then pedal into New Franklin, your final destination.

Franklin, the origin of the Santa Fe Trail, was founded in 1816. Named after Benjamin Franklin, it was located on a low floodplain on the Missouri River's north bank. It was from this town that William Becknell departed in 1821 for Santa Fe. Franklin was the teenaged Kit Carson's home until he left on a Santa Fe Trail wagon trek in 1826. Franklin was also the first outfitting center for traders who made their living on the trail.

Because of the Missouri River's ever-changing course, there were three towns in succession named Franklin. As the river overflowed, the towns relocated. The first Franklin, established in 1817, was prosperous and growing for about a decade. By 1818, it had one hundred and fifty houses. According to Gregory Franzwa in *The Santa Fe Trail Revisited,* the value of lots increased by more than 1,000 percent. According to an 1819 census, Franklin boasted four taverns, thirteen stores, two billiard rooms, a jail, a post office, and a weekly newspaper, the *Missouri Intelligencer.* However, despite its auspicious beginning, repeated flooding by the Missouri River brought the town's demise in 1828. Franklin Number One is now referred to as Old Franklin.

Franklin Number Two sprang up in 1826, when some of Old Franklin's residents relocated northeast to higher ground. Apparently the second town was too far from the Missouri River and its prosperous riverbank trading activity; consequently, it failed as well. Just a few years after its establishment, some dissatisfied residents moved a mile to the west, where they established still another Franklin. But even "just plain Franklin," which today is called "New Franklin," failed to grow. And yet at least it does remain today, with a population around 1,200.

Go to Broadway Avenue and the town's central commercial area. A large red boulder and plaque, put in place in 1909 by the DAR, is inscribed **The Beginning of the Trail.** For you, of course, it marks the "end" of your trail and over 1,000 miles from the Santa Fe Plaza's "beginning" of the trail marker.

New Franklin is a friendly place, where merchants and other residents will probably be more than happy to answer your questions. A short walk or bike ride around town should include the following:

The **Peter B. Harris–J. Warren Chilton Home**, 108 North Missouri, was built in 1832. This Federal style two-story brick home is listed on the National Register of Historic Places. During its restoration in 1947, the porch was added. This can be viewed from the outside only, as it is closed to the public.

The **Old Seminary**, dating from 1826, served as the first school in New Franklin. It replaced the Old Franklin Seminary that was torn down in the 1920s.

Such are the major highlights of New Franklin, but you may want to spend more time exploring this historic town before leaving your Santa Fe Trail adventure. Soon you will be packing up bicycle and gear and heading homeward by car or train. Don't be surprised if, like so many bygone Santa Fe Trail travelers, you find your way back again.

End of the Trail, New Franklin, Missouri.

CONCLUSION

CONCLUSION

As Susan Magoffin wrote in her 1846 diary, *Down the Santa Fe Trail and into Mexico*, "If exercise is good for one, surely you are benefited now." During her day, not only merchants but adventurers and ordinary folks were caught up in the romance, danger, and excitement of the trail. It was not a once-in-a-lifetime trip, but a place to return to again and again.

The history, the sweeping, expansive terrain, the people along the way, and the wonderful sense of fitness and personal well-being gained from covering so many miles on wheels are likely to remain with you for a lifetime. The travails of the trip—windy and/or rainy days; trucks that nearly swept you off narrow, shoulderless roads; fierce winds that blew from morning till night—these will fade with time.

Whether or not you go back in person to visit your favorite places along the route, you will no doubt return in your mind. You will never read or hear again about the Old West without being able to better relate to it. "Oh yes, I was there," you will tell yourself when hearing mention of Fort Dodge or Fort Union. Songs from the frontier will bring back vivid images of having cycled through that vast, lonely, inspiring terrain. And you may even find yourself trying to find an excuse to return to Trinidad, Council Grove, Lexington, or other towns along the Santa Fe Trail.

Despite 170 years of change, riding the trail offers today's adventurer-cyclist the opportunity to pedal back through an important chapter of United States history, to share some of the adventures— and misadventures—of our pioneer forebears, and to finish the journey on the riverbank at New Franklin, Missouri, launching point for six decades of trade and adventure. As Susan Magoffin suggested, you will be benefited in many ways, one of which may be a feeling of respect and affection for those who went before you. ✺

Following are campsites and chambers of commerce for the towns along the route. A very few special hotels are listed because of historical interest. For more hotel listings or special sightseeing information, contact the chambers of commerce.

ARROW ROCK, MISSOURI

Office Administrator
Arrow Rock State Historic Site
Arrow Rock, MO 65320
(816) 837-3330
200-acre camping area overlooking the Missouri River. Modern restrooms with showers. Over 40 campsites available on a first-come, first-served basis. Between $5 and $11 depending on season and facilities. Lovely, grassy; lots of trees.

Arrow Rock Lyceum
Arrow Rock, MO 65320
(816) 837-3331 for theatre performances

BALDWIN CITY, KANSAS

Douglas State Fishing Lake and Campground
County road 2½ miles northeast of town.
RV and tent camping; pit toilets; tables; boating; rowboat rentals.

Baldwin City Chamber of Commerce
Baldwin City, KS 66006
(913) 594-3200

CIMARRON, NEW MEXICO

Rogers RV Campground
Main Street
Cimarron, NM 87714
(505) 376-2406
Laundry; showers; ample campsites; no cooking facilities.

St. James Hotel
Rt. 1, Box 2
Main Street
Cimarron, NM 87714
(505) 376-2664

Cimarron Chamber of Commerce
Cimarron, NM 87714
(505) 376-2417

COUNCIL GROVE, KANSAS

Council Grove Lake
Army Corps of Engineers
Rt. 2, Box 110
Council Grove, KS 66846
Write or call (316) 757-5195 for reservations.
Eight campsites around the lake.

Richey Cove
On Hwy. 177, 1½ miles north of the junction of highways 56 and 177.
50 campsites; security; showers; cooking facilities.
Fees vary from $7 to $11.

Council Grove Chamber of Commerce
313 W. Main St.
Council Grove, KS 66846
(316) 767-5413

DODGE CITY, KANSAS

Water Sports Campground
500 Cherry St.
Dodge City, KS 67801
(316) 225-9325 or 225-9003

Dodge City Convention and Visitors Department
P.O. Box 1474
Dodge City, KS 67801
(316) 225-8186

FORT UNION, NEW MEXICO

P.O. Box 127
Watrous, NM 87753
(505) 425-8025

HILLSBORO, KANSAS

Hillsboro City Park
South Birch Street

Marion Lake
Elizabeth Birkey (316) 947-3506
Police (316) 947-3162

Hillsboro Chamber of Commerce
109 S. Main
Hillsboro, KS 67063
(316) 947-3506

INDEPENDENCE, MISSOURI

Reorganized Church of Jesus Christ of Latter Day
Saints (RLDS) Camp
406 S. Pleasant
Independence, MO 64051
(816) 833-4300 for reservations

Independence Chamber of Commerce
P.O. Box 1077
Independence, MO 64051
(816) 252-4745

LA JUNTA, COLORADO

KOA Campground
(719) 384-9580
Two miles west of La Junta on U.S. 50.
Showers; store; laundromat.

Koshare Indian Museum
115 W. Eighteenth St.
P.O. Box 580
La Junta, CO 81050
(719) 384-4411

La Junta Chamber of Commerce
P. O. Box 408
La Junta, CO 81050
(719) 384-7411

LAKIN, KANSAS

Beymer Park
Rt. 50, 3 miles south of town.
Showers available.

Kearny County Museum
P.O. Box 329
Lakin, KS 67860
Write or call Lakin City Administrator
(316) 355-6252 or (316) 355-7448 for information.

LAMAR, COLORADO

KOA Campground
3 miles west of Lamar on Hwy. 50.

Lamar Chamber of Commerce
109-A E. Beech St.
Lamar, CO 81052
Police (719) 336-4341
Sheriff (719) 336-3234

LARNED, KANSAS

Schnack Park
1st and Carroll
Larned, KS 67550
(316) 285-6916
Contact police before staying there (316) 285-3188.

Larned Chamber of Commerce
P.O. Box 240
Larned, KS 67550
(316) 285-6916

Santa Fe Trail Association
Sec.-Treas.
RR 3
Larned, KS 67550

LAS VEGAS, NEW MEXICO

Dean of Students
Office of Student Affairs
New Mexico Highlands University
Las Vegas, NM 87701
(505) 454-3590

KOA Campground
5 miles south of Las Vegas I-25, Exit 339.
Quiet; shady; pool and game room.
(505) 454-0180

Las Vegas Chamber of Commerce
P.O. Box 148

Las Vegas, NM 87701
(505) 425-8631

Plaza Hotel
230 on the Old Town Plaza
Las Vegas, NM 87701
(505) 425-3591

LEXINGTON, MISSOURI

Lexington City Park
Park Drive

Lexington Chamber of Commerce
Main Street
Lexington, MO 64067
(816) 259-3082

NEW FRANKLIN, MISSOURI

New Franklin City Park
From Hwy. 5, take a left on Broadway, go to Union St.
and take a right turn. A short road takes you directly
to the park. Campsites with water and picnic area.

New Franklin Chamber of Commerce
New Franklin City Hall
Broadway Street
(816) 848-2288

SANTA FE, NEW MEXICO

Apache Canyon RV Camp
(505) 982-1419 or call Mike Pitel (505) 827-7400
I-25, Exit 294

Santa Fe County Chamber of Commerce
510 N. Guadalupe
Santa Fe, NM 87501
(505) 983-7317

Santa Fe Trail Association (see Larned, Kansas).

STERLING, KANSAS

Sterling Lake
Corner of Van Buren and First on east
side of Broadway.
Campsites available; no reservations needed;
picnic area; shelters; no showers.

Sterling City Clerk
P. O. Box 287
Sterling, KS 67579
(316) 278-3423

TRINIDAD, COLORADO

Trinidad State Recreation Area
Trinidad/ Las Animas County

Chamber of Commerce
309 Nevada Ave.
Trinidad, CO 81082
(719) 846-9285

WAGON MOUND, NEW MEXICO

Town has two truck stops, one 2-unit motel.

LJM Travel Center
(505) 666-2364
Old Hwy. 85, just off I-25
on the way into Wagon Mound.
Two rooms available.

Trailer Park—Frank S. Pino
(505) 666-2430
South of town on old U. S. Hwy. 85
by Craftmasters Cabinet Shop.
Can pitch tents; water available; no showers.

Village of Wagon Mound
City Clerk's Office
P. O. Box 87
Wagon Mound, NM 87752
(505) 666-2408
Larger groups may arrange with city clerk to
stay in Wagon Mound School's gymnasium. Call or
write ahead to the city clerk.

For information about Willard Chilcott's Santa Fe
Trail Bicycle Trek, contact:
Willard Chilcott, 885 Camino del Este, Santa Fe, NM
87501, (505) 982-1282.

SELECTED REFERENCES

Bryan, Howard. *Wildest of the Wild West: True Tales of a Frontier Town on the Santa Fe Trail*. Santa Fe: Clear Light Publishers, 1991.

Franzwa, Gregory M. *The Santa Fe Trail Revisited*. St. Louis: The Patrice Press, 1989.

Gregg, Josiah. *Commerce of the Prairies*. 1844. Reprint. Edited by Max L. Moorhead. Norman: University of Oklahoma Press, 1990.

Lavender, David. *The Trail to Santa Fe*. Santa Fe: Trails West Publishing, 1989.

Leonard, Zenas. *Leonard's Narrative: Adventures of Zenas Leonard, Fur Trader and Trapper 1831-1836*. Edited by W.F. Wagner. Cleveland: Burroughs Brothers, 1904.

Magoffin, Susan Shelby. *Down the Santa Fe Trail and into Mexico: The Diary of Susan Shelby Magoffin, 1846-1847*. Edited by Stella Drumm. Lincoln: University of Nebraska Press, 1982.

Mays, Buddy. *Ancient Cities of the Southwest: A Practical Guide to the Major Prehistoric Ruins of Arizona, New Mexico, Utah, and Colorado*. San Francisco: Chronicle Books, 1990.

Pike, Zebulon M. *The Journals of Zebulon Montgomery Pike, 1779-1813*, with letters and related documents, Vol. 1. Norman: University of Oklahoma Press, 1966.

Sappington, John. *The Theory and Treatment of Fevers*. Published by the author. Revised by Ferinando Smith. Arrow Rock, Missouri.

Simmons, Marc. *Following the Santa Fe Trail: A Guide for Modern Travelers*. Santa Fe: Ancient City Press, 1984, 1986.

———. *On the Santa Fe Trail*. Lawrence: University of Kansas Press, 1986.

Sloane, Eugene A. *Sloane's Handy Pocket Guide to Bicycle Repair*. New York: Fireside Books/division of Simon & Schuster, 1988.

———. *Sloane's New Bicycle Maintenance Manual*. New York: Fireside Books/division of Simon & Schuster, 1991.

Stocking, Hobart E. *The Road to Santa Fe*. New York: Hastings House Publishers, 1971.

Sutton, Remar. "Who Needs a Helmet?" *Reader's Digest*, May 1991, 107-110.

Udall, Stewart. *In Coronado's Footsteps*. Tucson: Southwest Parks and Monuments Association, 1991.

Van der Plas, Rob. *The Bicycle Touring Manual: Using the Bike for Touring and Camping*. San Francisco: Bicycle Books, 1988.

———. *The Bicycle Repair Book: Maintaining and Repairing the Modern Bicycle*. San Francisco: Bicycle Books, 1991.

———. *Roadside Bicycle Repairs: The Simple Guide to Fixing Your Bike*. 2nd ed. San Francisco: Bicycle Books, 1990.

Bold page numbers indicate photographs

151